GET OUT OF YOUR HIDING PLACE

SAULO SANTOS

GET OUT OF YOUR HIDING PLACE

IT'S TIME TO START LIVING GOD'S DREAM

Hope2u Publishing House

"Get out of your hiding place: It's time to start living God's dream"

Translated from the Portuguese, "Saia do seu esconderijo: É tempo de viver os sonhos de Deus"

© 2021 by Saulo Oliveira Santos

First published in Great Britain in 2023 by HOPE2u Publishing House.

The right of Saulo Oliveira Santos to be identified as the Author of the Work has been asserted by him in accordance with the Copyright, Designs and Patents Act 1988.

1

First edition March 2023

Proofreading/Editing by Clare Irwin (Cre8tion Studios)
Revision by Louise Matoso Santos
Translation, Art and Typewriting by Saulo Oliveira Santos
Cover Photo by Ante Hamersmit on Unsplash

A CIP catalogue record for this title is available from the British Library

Hardback ISBN 979-8-831499-40-7
Paperback ISBN 979-8-831494-66-2

Hope2u Publishing House Ltd
www.hope2u.co.uk

For Lillian,
Who never stopped believing in me,
even when I did…

FOREWORD

My second son by birth, Saulo Santos, is one of the rare Christians who are not satisfied by the type of monotonous Christian life that translates into a lifeless, formal religion. Many live it and are reduced to only participating in services, complying with commandments and doing what is politically correct.

My son's life has been marked by seasons that raised him to be a Christian beyond his time, reminiscent of "the great cloud of witnesses" of biblical history. Who knows, maybe, in the spiritual realms, his name is not "Saulo" (the one asked for), but Paul (small) because that's how he feels in comparison to Christ and His work.

I want to start by telling you about one of the most significant episodes which launched Saulo on his journey towards success in both the secular and the spiritual life.

At the age of two, Saulo was a quiet child who rarely complained, despite the problem he had had since babyhood, that he couldn't keep milk down well and frequently suffered from colic. At two years old he already had a good vocabulary, but he chose to speak in monosyllables and appeared quiet and sad. Saulo barely slept, didn't feed well and didn't speak.

One Sunday morning, we had arrived back from a service at the evangelical church we attended at the time. My wife was trying to feed Saulo his bottle when he closed his teeth, tensed his arms and legs, and fainted. Our lack of experience as parents meant that we hadn't noticed he was running a high fever. Thankfully we lived about a block away from a hospital in São Paulo at that time.

We ran there, and they found he had a fever of more than 40ºC. The seizure had been caused by a high temperature. Events then took a traumatic turn when, despite the effort of doctors and nurses, he didn't come round and the doctors' concern started mounting.

I decided to stay in the room and watch everything while my wife remained in the waiting room, desperately crying and praying. We knew that it was no coincidence that that morning she had read the story of

Lazarus's resurrection and now, in despair, she cried out for the Lord to resurrect her son.

The situation in the room didn't change and I also started to pray, saying: "My God, my son's life belongs to you anyway, but I ask you to save him". Every parent knows only too well the neurologic side effects that a seizure can bring when it goes on for too long. All of a sudden, after this prayer, Saulo came round and the doctors were able to treat him. It was hard, but we had to leave him at the hospital overnight, without us.

The next morning, he was released from hospital. When we went to fetch him we gave his name to the nurse, who replied, "Oh, that chatty little boy, the one who doesn't stop talking for a minute!" My wife said, "No, that can't be him, my son doesn't talk"; Saulo left that place like a new child, he was extroverted, chatty, joyful, singing and dancing. A new little Saulo.

I do have a lot more to tell you about him, but let me just say that as he grew, there were more and more miracles. It was as if his life was marked by the Lord from a young age. The book "Get out of your hiding place" reflects what our God can do in a human life, how He watches out for every little detail and prepares purpose in a person to mark their generation.

As we analyse the lives of men and women of God whom God touched and used in the Bible, we can see how all of them went through trials, defeats and victories.

But we can also see the spiritual growth necessary for them to get out of their hiding place, for them to become useful in the plans of the Almighty upon the earth. For example, Lazarus was dead, but Jesus called him by name and said, "Lazarus, come out!".

In other words, it was as if God said to Saulo too, "Get out of your tomb, out of your hiding place!". What was Lazarus's purpose, his calling? It was to be alive and to be a witness to the miracle the Lord can do in someone's life!

I want to finish by encouraging you to read on. This book will help you to experience more from God in your life and serve him at the opportune time. Let the Holy Spirit light up every word and every paragraph.

Tirso de Mello Santos
October 2021
Ponta Grossa, Brazil

PREFACE

This book has taken me a decade to write. It has been maturing inside me and following me on my journey of getting to know God and walking with Him in the ministry. Each lesson contained in it is very precious to me and was learned amidst joys and tears. Everything I have learnt is a fruit of God's immense mercy and grace over me.

I have often been ministered to and comforted while reading and re-reading these pages. I have also been inspired to find my way back, and to continuously move towards what God has planned for me.

I'm very grateful for the opportunity of extending this gift I've received from God to you. I believe with all my heart that if God can do something with my life, He can certainly do something in yours too.

I hope you find inspiration in these pages and strength, but also the challenge you need right now in your walk with God. Even if the days we're living in are evil, there's a glorious future before us if we decide to believe and walk the path He has prepared.

Like the sower who throws the seed, I pray that this message may touch your heart and bear much fruit.

Saulo Santos
October 2021
Cardiff, Wales

INTRODUCTION

As a pastor's son, God's calling had always been a familiar subject to me. Many pastors' children see in the life and ministry of their parents a stumbling block or something oppressive, hypocritical even. I never did though. I don't think I had either the time or the opportunity to think like that.

In fact, when my parents got born again, I was about five years old, and contrary to what most adults think, I already had a keen awareness of what was going on around me. I could see my family transitioning from darkness into light. I could see how our home, once entirely defeated by the lack of peace, became a place of life that would bless many other families in its turn.

Serving God became the reason for my parents' existence; it became their passion and their constant pursuit. I believe that one of the greatest crises that a child can face is when their parents are not truthful or when they appear to be something they are not. On the other hand, when parents are fully committed and passionate about something, with no holding back, reservations or limits, and they are genuine and dedicated, body and soul, there's no external factor that will overshadow it in their child's heart.

The passion for the presence of God in my parents' lives became my passion. Their pursuit became mine. Their purpose, their vocation and calling became mine too.

From an early age, I have been dedicated to finding out the purposes of God for my own life. Then, also from an early age, I chose to get involved in the service of this loving and wonderful God who had changed the course of our lives forever.

My family was always passionate about music, so serving God in this context was just natural. Amongst a family of composers, maestros, virtuoso musicians, singers and poets, I also have become entirely involved in this captivating service. Yet, far beyond the enjoyment of the music alone, we've seen the power of God manifesting itself mightily.

I grew up ministering music and worship to the Lord, and I witnessed a revival in the Church as it grew and matured in my country, Brazil. What I witnessed were repercussions of the spiritual movements that had broken out in Argentina and also later in Canada. I've lived through an apostolic revival that God has been pouring out in the last decades. Today, I am a witness again of a revival breaking out in the United Kingdom.

Serving God is my passion, my heart and my calling and my search to know God's plan and his purposes for my life started long ago. Indeed, finding out about God's will and fulfilling His plans was always a recurrent theme of conversation in my family, since my childhood.

However, many concepts, values, and incorrect beliefs that I had built muddled me when I was trying to pursue my vocation in the Lord. I know today that I placed many of my preconceptions like moulds, expecting God to pour into them what he wanted to do in my life.

Even though I was very dedicated to reaching my target, the more I built my life based solely on what I thought, the further I drifted from the path God had prepared for me. And I wasn't even aware of it.

In some ways my story started to resemble that of "Jonah", the prophet. The Bible tells us that Jonah received a specific calling from God, but he decided to go the opposite way instead. Jonah didn't seem to care if the people perished or not. In fact, he seemed much more interested in his own fate than in anybody else's.

Jonah had been dedicated to seeking God and he was a servant of the Lord. Still, like many of us, he spent time wandering off the path before he eventually hit the target.

There are many things that can make us retreat in the face of God's calling, such as a simple lack of knowledge or distraction. We might even think we're not able to do it or that we deserve a higher badge of honour. Also, we might think we're too good or too bad to do anything at all, or it might be something else. Whatever it is, we can find ourselves behaving exactly like Jonah, going in the opposite direction to God's calling and his plans for us.

In my personal experience, taking into account my abilities and the things I would think I was good enough to do, I thought it was natural that God would call me to work as a minister of music and worship. After all, the skills and the inclination were already "in my blood", so it was just comfortable to accept this responsibility.

In the meantime, any other things God might have wanted me to do I would have considered taboo or just downright impossible. My reasons, I thought, were justified as, after all, I simply didn't have the skills.

Evangelisation, for example, came right at the top of that list. It was simply impossible for anybody to convince me to put any effort whatsoever in that direction. Although I felt free to express myself through music, I am a very reserved individual. I don't like confrontation, so speaking in public, preaching the Gospel, or even worse, to a non-believer, was something just impossible to someone of my nature.

I've always run from evangelisation with all my strength. Just the thought of approaching a total stranger, talking about God's love and inviting him to salvation would make me blush. Time after time, opportunity after opportunity, I kept having to create more and more excuses to run away from what I would classify as "not my calling".

However "justified" my reasons were, however sincere I was before God when making myself available for his service, when I would say "here I am", the fear of witnessing was paralysing. I could get involved in any supporting role in evangelistic events, even better if related to music. Still, I would never get involved with the evangelistic task itself.

Jonah ran to Tarshish. And Tarshish means, literally, "wealth". So Jonah ran towards what was good for him, towards what was nice and pleasant, towards the things that could bring him some benefit. In other words, what Jonah really wanted was to stay in his comfort zone and not leave it by any means.

Many of us do that constantly and maybe we don't even notice. We remain so attached to the defence of our comfort zone and repeat the same excuses so many times that we start believing in them. Based on my own opinions and experiences, I had told myself so many times that evangelism was not my calling that I piously started to believe in it.

But who are we to say to God what we should do or not? Is not God the one who calls us? Is it not Him who chooses us? Who am I to say who can or who can't do something? Who am I to determine which way I should go? Jeremiah spoke about this. "O LORD, I know the way of man is not in himself; It is not in man who walks to direct his own steps."[1] God is God, and He has the right to choose whom He wants to do what He wants to do.

The Lord does not choose as we choose. Indeed, He seems to look for the most improbable candidates. When Samuel went to anoint one of the older brothers of David, God stopped him: "But the LORD said to Samuel, 'Do not look at his appearance or at his physical stature, because I have refused him. For the LORD does not see as man sees; for man looks at the outward appearance, but the LORD looks at the heart.'"[2]

---

1 Jeremiah 10:23 NKJV.

2 1 Samuel 16:7 NKJV.

Despite all of the biblical examples, we, as men, continue stubbornly thinking that our personal skills matter! In addition to making ourselves the judge of others, we judge ourselves and refrain from doing what God asks us to because we insist on thinking that we don't have the right abilities or the right conditions to do it in.

David was an improbable candidate. Samuel, too; in fact, he would not even have been born if it wasn't for a miraculous intervention from God. Solomon was an unlikely choice, Paul too; in addition to everything, he even persecuted the Church. We could do this all day, finding example after example, and we'd see that God constantly chooses those who are unworthy or even those who had decided to give up on the things that appeared to have some value.

I am an improbable candidate; you are also possibly the least probable candidate for the work that God has called you to do.

Jonah didn't only run to a comfort zone, but he also invested money and resources in the project. The Bible tells us that he paid a fee to board the ship. We do the same when, in addition to not pursuing the Lord's projects and plans, we spend our resources (time, money, thoughts and dreams) on projects that our exclusively "ours", projects that can guarantee us a longer stay in the comfort zone.

Another thing to note is that Jonah was so absorbed by his plan to escape and seek his comfort zone that he didn't give up, even when he faced tremendous adversity. The scripture tells us that he even asked to be thrown out of the boat. Jonah could have repented right there but was effectively saying, "You can throw me out the boat because I'd prefer to die than do what God has called me to do!".

Jonah's escape seemed relentless, but I see God's great mercy and grace in this example because God didn't give up on Jonah, even in the face of his stubbornness. I thank God because He hasn't given up on me either and if you are still alive, God hasn't given up on you! If you choose today to surrender and seek His will, He is full of grace and mercy to put you back in the right direction.

Even if he was in the unpleasant situation of being slowly digested, after being swallowed by the fish, Jonah still took three days to repent and decide to do what God had called him to do. Jonah went to the furthest limit of his own stubbornness while insisting on disobeying God.

I always had the desire to fulfil God's will and seek his plans. One day I realised, though, I was directly opposing his will. I was just ignoring what God was calling me to do.

I was only able to surrender when God interrupted my plans and placed me in a crisis, from which I realised it was impossible to fight against Him. In that, my eyes were open, and I could see the reality of my situation. With a new job offer that didn't consolidate, a possibility of moving abroad that didn't happen, in the blink of an eye, I was brought down from my stable situation into having no perspective whatsoever.

In finding our path again, my wife and I decided to establish ourselves in Ponta Grossa[3] and serve God in that town. We have seen God's favour there, blowing in our direction, and doors that would seem impossible (housing, job and ministry) have opened, consolidating without a doubt that God was leading us to that place.

Crises have this unique ability to get us to question all our values, plans, and concepts regarding life and God's service. They lead us to seek the Lord with an attitude of surrender that would be impossible in any other circumstance. Our plans, values and concepts stop us from seeing clearly, just like they did to Jonah, and only when there's nothing left can we see the reality of our condition.

To my surprise, God has called us for the task of evangelisation. Against all the odds and defying all our limits, God has been teaching us to depend totally on him. In this book, I want to share the discoveries I've been making in God about life, calling and ministry, which are helping me move forward in this walk.

---

3 TN: A city in the state of Parana, in Brazil.

I've read books by authors I respect very much that teach about the calling of God. Still, some of these books argue that your calling might as well be the things you are already knowledgeable about and able. While that might be the experience of many, I cannot agree entirely because my experience is the direct opposite.

Like Jonah, I was going in the opposite direction, with the excuse of being inadequate. Maybe you have another reason while also running away from what God has called you to do. Or perhaps you are not a fugitive, but you are in the process of fulfilling your calling.

Regardless of your situation, I believe that this book's content will help you find the hope, encouragement, faith, and clarity you need to continue your walk towards the purpose of God in your life.

WEAKNESS

I recently read an article about an Icelandic actor and athlete who broke a weight lifting record. This young man, Hafthór Björnsson, at only twenty-six years old, was able to carry a ten-meter tree log, weighing six hundred and fifty kilograms, for five steps.

The legend tells us the former record holder was a Viking called Orm Storulfsson. In the ninth or the tenth century, he walked three steps carrying a log weighing six hundred and fifty kilograms. It took ten other mere mortals to put the log on his back. The story didn't end well for Orm, however, as after the third step, his back broke under the immense pressure.

Happily, Hafthór didn't break his back, and today he holds the title of "The World's Strongest Viking"[4].

This example might seem somewhat radical, but it illustrates the fact that people are different and have different capacities and limits. When I see a news article like this, I usually compare the achievement in question with my own abilities and limitations. My personal weight lifting record is undoubtedly not even close to the record achieved by this champion. A feat of this kind results from many years of focus and preparation and still remains beyond most of us. It even ended disastrously for the former champion who overstepped his limits. When he tried to go beyond what he could do, despite his strength and preparation, it wasn't enough, and the damage caused was irreparable. Indeed, there will be other champions who'll achieve even more incredible things in our generation and generations to come. Nevertheless, we all have our own physical limitations, even if they are different for every person.

Beyond physical limitations, we also have limitations in our soul, that is, our emotions, will, and thoughts. Such limits can be a lot more paralysing than any physical limitation. For example, if we say in our hearts that we

---

4 Mail Online News; http://www.dailymail.co.uk/news/
article-2939595/Game-Thrones-actor-played-Mountain-World-s-
Strongest-Viking-smashes-1-000-year-old-record-carrying-1-433lbs-
log.html; accessed on 5/5/2015.

will never or are incapable of doing something, we will certainly never do it, whether or not we have the capacity to do so. Just like it's written: "For as he thinks in his heart, so is he"[5].

If we guide our lives according to the opinions of our soul, we are indeed at risk of creating limitations that don't actually exist or of blocking our own advance as individuals and sons of God.

During my life, I have seen people saying they cannot speak in public, or others saying that they don't have the capacity to learn a new skill, a foreign language or a musical instrument, for example. And even if they did lack the talents or the skills, they could have acquired them. It was their thoughts, will and emotions (that is, their soul) that had become their real limiter.

The prophet Jeremiah warned us: "The heart is deceitful above all things, and desperately wicked; who can know it?"[6] Our soul can and will undoubtedly deceive us. Our thoughts, will and emotions are, in their essence, liars and perverse, so they become the true enemies of our plans.

Some people struggle with trauma from the past, while others cannot forgive someone. Some are battling mental health issues, like depression, and some suffer

---

5 Proverbs 23:7 NKJV.

6 Jeremiah 17:9 NKJV.

from guilt. Others are troubled with feelings of inadequacy or incapacity. Some struggle to get over bad habits, addictions and compulsions. Anyway, the list goes on and on. I believe that all of us can relate, one way or the other, with the limits of our souls.

These negative feelings and thoughts will not always be the only things to prevent us from reaching all our potential. Often, our own will is the enemy. What we truly want will be expressed in our actions.

I can say that I need a spiritual revival, but my actions and priorities will reveal what my real intentions are and even if my mouth declares itself in favour, what I actually do will expose what my real will is. So it might also be that my will, my real will, also becomes a limitation to me.

Finally, I think that maybe one of the most terrible things is when we hear somebody making fatalistic declarations like "this is the way it is", or "that's impossible", or catchphrases like "a leopard can't change its spots"[7], or "God made me this way, and I'll die this way". By doing this our own words reduce, conform and enslave us to our own limitations and weaknesses.

All those wishing to seek and fulfil God's will in their lives and their generation will face obstacles and the first

---

7 TN: The original expression reads "pau que nasce torto, morre torto", which translates to "a stick that is born crooked dies crooked".

obstacles will be within themselves, in the form of limitations and weaknesses. In fact, these limitations and weaknesses won't be our enemies in the beginning only but will be closer and present throughout our faith journey.

If we take just a few examples from the Bible, we will see Moses, a condemned criminal who struggled to speak, became a leader, legislator and prophet. He not only freed the people of God from slavery but also left us a priceless legacy in the Old Testament scriptures.

Then there's Gideon, who considered himself the least of all from the least of all tribes and hid like a coward but then stood up as a mighty and courageous man, just as God had said he would.

Then there's David, the young shepherd boy who became the nation's king. In spite of his many mistakes, God called David a man after His own heart.

Jonah, went against his mission and followed a path of death, but the grace of the Lord shone upon him, bringing him back and throwing him back into His purpose.

If there's anything in common among these characters, it's that they all had many defects and weaknesses. All of them had limitations that seemed impassable. However, they all attained a lot more than they could ever have imagined. In a similar way, God's work and calling may seem impossible for many of us. In our souls, we may imagine being inept, unable and unworthy. We may also have opposing ideas or simply want to do something else.

This kind of mindset may leave us thinking that we need to improve a lot before God can use us. In extreme cases, these ideas can also lead to frustration or even cause us to give up entirely. Our ecclesiastical tradition may let us think this way, but if we consider the biblical examples, God doesn't seem worried about candidates' CVs in the same way that we do. In all honesty, we would certainly not choose as he chooses. Indeed, we would look for people with impeccable CVs, who had never failed, possessing great eloquence and erudition.

While thinking about all of this, I understood something that changed my perspective. We usually think that our weaknesses are our absolute limit, the end of the line. Since that's where our abilities end, we believe that to be a point we could never cross.

Although we might not believe it, the truth is that our weaknesses and limitations are not "the end" but rather the pre-requisite for our calling. When we consider the Church's history and remember the men and women of God from the past, we tend to see them as "great". We even mention them as the "great men of God" or "great women of God".

We tend to consider them as some different kind of human beings, with superhuman abilities, with extraordinary motivation, an out of this world perseverance and a life of prayer so intense that they might even be referred to as legendary.

We imagine these people as human beings free from temptation, free from weakness, free from dismay, free from the passions of this world. So, ultimately, we consider them as a unique group of people separated by God for a greater purpose. We think they must have received a superior measure of grace to glorify God in their generation, make history and be an example for the rest of us.

So, let's take one example, Paul, the apostle to the gentiles. When we think about Paul, we imagine in our hearts a courageous preacher, evangelist and missionary, a man that undoubtedly lived his life in such a way as to transform the world.

We think about the great Paul who performed extraordinary acts for God, who preached the Gospel with boldness and endured many afflictions. A man who didn't let himself stop because of the cold, hunger, lack of comfort, threats, compliments, whipping, prisons, or anything. Paul established churches and wrote a good part of the New Testament by the Holy Spirit, and his writings are a challenge to all Bible scholars until this day.

From this perspective, Paul looks a lot more talented and skilled than the rest of us. He appears to have received a more remarkable ability than all other human beings to further the work of the Gospel. However, this kind of thinking couldn't be further from the truth.

Of course Paul had many natural skills, but he regarded all of them as useless. So Paul denied all he had, everything that could make him stand out as a human being, all of his scientific and religious knowledge, and considered them "loss so that he could gain Christ"[8].

Some translations of the Bible even use the word "manure", emphasising how Paul decided to regard everything he represented. He considered everything worthless, useless, not worth keeping, and only good for throwing away. In this sense, all arguments for Paul's superior talents giving him an advantage are shattered.

We all developed skills and became qualified for many things; we obtained knowledge, wisdom in life, professional experience, etc. And all these things are great, and together they form our whole life experience. Likewise, we can all point out our own weaknesses and strengths. Each one of us can tell what our qualities and defects are. We all know what we can and what we can't do. We all have strengths, but we all have weaknesses too. We know the limitations our humanity imposes on us.

---

8 "What is more, I consider everything a loss because of the surpassing worth of knowing Christ Jesus my Lord, for whose sake I have lost all things. I consider them garbage, that I may gain Christ", Philippians 3:8.

The same "great apostle" Paul, that we talked about just now, who had so many reasons to "boast in the flesh", that is, to be proud of himself, said this: "Therefore I will boast all the more gladly about my weaknesses, so that Christ's power may rest on me."[9]

Paul had weaknesses, which puts him in the same category as us. He was a normal human being who battled against the same weaknesses as we do. So, in the same manner that weaknesses limit you and me, Paul was also limited by them.

This might seem a little scandalous to say but I think that Paul was weak from the beginning of his life until the end of it. All the weaknesses Paul had when he was born again remained in Paul until the end of his life. Paul was and always had been weak and even said it himself.

He asked God to remove his "thorn in his flesh"[10]; something in his human and flesh nature afflicted him, and he wanted to see it cut out and changed. We idealise characters like Paul as flawless, which leads us to believe that the problem could never be them, it should be something external. The idea that men called by God are infal-

---

9 2 Corinthians 12:9.

10 "And lest I should be exalted above measure by the abundance of the revelations, a thorn in the flesh was given to me, a messenger of Satan to buffet me, lest I be exalted above measure.", 2 Corinthians 12:7 NKJV.

lible and perfect is widespread, but nothing could be further from the truth or more opposed to the Gospel.

Anyway, if we leave aside all theological debate of what this could really mean, let's note that a thorn in somebody's flesh is something that profoundly hurts and disturbs them. Divinely inspired, Paul doesn't write about his problem in explicit terms, but while he does it generically, he includes us all. You and I may not have the same exact problem Paul had, but we can all relate to having something in ourselves that hurts and disturbs us profoundly, such as a "thorn in the flesh".

If we apply this example to us today, what do we have in ourselves that we can't overcome? What is there in our nature that may disturb us? Just like Paul had his weaknesses, you and I have ours. Interestingly, God didn't answer Paul's wishes to remove the thorn, yet He said His grace was enough for Paul. So likewise, God doesn't say he will remove our weakness, yet in our weakness, the power of God will be made perfect.[11]

Paul discovered something in God's grace that made him declare he would rejoice in his weaknesses and be proud of being weak. This perspective may actually be the most significant difference between Paul and most of us.

---

11 "But he said to me, 'My grace is sufficient for you, for my power is made perfect in weakness.'", 2 Corinthians 12:9a.

Usually, the things that we know how to do give us joy. We rejoice in all the things we have education, training and preparation for; all our courses, our degrees, our specialisation, our MBAs, our master degrees, our doctorate degrees, our post-doctorate degrees, etc. Therefore, we feel confident to act and work only in these things we know, which are our joy and strength.

On the other hand, our limitations are reasons for sadness, and our weaknesses make us feel overthrown. So the things we consider to be our limitations, we place behind a wall and we feel silently resigned to the fact that they prevent us from pursuing certain paths. Hence, you and I may think that we cannot do certain things, so our instinct will be to run away from every opportunity that presses us into them.

I was never, for example, very interested in sports, nobody in my family is. It might seem strange to a lot of people but, in spite of growing up in Brazil, I wasn't bothered about football. The other kids would always take me by surprise when asking which football club I supported.

For me, playing sports was an obligation to be carried out. As I didn't care much and wasn't very good at it, I would avoid it at all costs. I didn't want to embarrass myself more than necessary. And that's what I did throughout high school, dodging physical education classes as much as possible.

That's how we deal with these issues. If there's something easy to do, and if we feel prepared enough, strong enough and comfortable enough with the task, we promptly accept the challenge and throw ourselves into the assignment ahead of us, which gives us joy. However, if we feel limited, unprepared, weak or uncomfortable, we will run away from it, which gives us sorrow.

Paul knew the things he had been educated and trained for, but he called them "manure", despising and neglecting them rather than claiming any joy in them. When it came to his limitations and weaknesses, however, everything that could stop him and prevent him from conquering, these things he called his glory, his greatest joy.

Paul's thoughts seem to run in the opposite direction to those of every other human being. Paul regarded his weakness as a reason for joy and simply disregarded everything else. All the things you and I hold as most precious, our reasons for joy, Paul regarded as totally worthless.

Some people may say, for example, that they cannot speak in public. Although sometimes it's not evident to an external observer, limitations are usually accompanied by sadness. While having a desire to serve God, they think that they can never do that particular thing. They think it's the end of the road. Or, maybe, they believe that God would not call them to do anything that would require public speaking since they are not, after all, any good at it.

This thought implies that God could only call us to do what we are qualified and skilled for. With this mindset, I could think that if I'm good at something, it's reasonable for God to call me for that, but if I'm not good enough, then it's impossible for God to do so. So we take our CVs to God and apply for the job we think we're good at. We put our strengths in evidence and hide our weaknesses. Then, foolishly, we believe that God thinks the same as we do.

Our weaknesses can be of different orders. Some struggle with addictions and compulsions, for example. Having tried to overcome them and having failed miserably, several times even, they might feel defeated and unable to handle their limitation. Finally, feeling profoundly sad, they give up the fight and never try again.

Some struggle with eating habits. Time after time, Monday after Monday, they start a diet and fail to get results even against their very first goals. If a diet is hard, they think that fasting will be impossible. Many give up on even trying to get over this weakness.

There are, of course, many other examples we could talk about, like the love of money, greed, infidelity, lousy time management, mood variations, sleeping, laziness and so many other things.

The exact nature of our struggles doesn't matter, these weaknesses will try to stop us, hinder us, and will constantly sadden and frustrate us. While preparing the most elaborate excuses, we will miss out on experiences we will never have and things we will never get involved with.

However, contrary to what we consider normal, weakness became Paul's joy. Can you imagine this? What did Paul discover in God that he got to the point of saying he was glad about the things that made him weak?

What is my weakness?

To understand our weaknesses, let's separate them into two big groups.

The first one I would call "weak weaknesses". In this group, I would include everything that I don't know, the things I can't do or think I can't do, or that, by my own will, I decide I don't want to do. Those are the things I would recognise as my weaknesses and limitations. Those are the things I run from.

It's also a typical behaviour not to admit such weaknesses and keep them secret. They seem like bridges we should never cross, secrets nobody should ever know. Around them we set a red alert, a sign, an alarm in our minds and hearts, saying: "Do not cross!".

We'll make excuses about these and avoid them, e.g. "I don't know how to… what will people think about me when they see me fail?", "This is not my calling", or, "This is for the young people", and finally, "Since I can't do it, I will finance someone who can". This is just a handful of the many other excuses we know and use.

This group includes all sorts of negative inclinations of the soul, like unbelief, unforgiveness, addictions, impure thoughts, gluttony, greed, lies, laziness, sleep, loneliness, sadness, depression, fear, etc. The list is, indeed, comprehensive.

In this group, we could also include feeling weak as a result of certain situations, like external pressure, loss, disease, financial crisis, family crisis, etc. In such circumstances, we tend to stop and do nothing. We tend to let ourselves be consumed by sadness and depression and be guided by what our feelings say.

Let's call the second group, (rather ironically) "strong weaknesses". In this group, I would include all the things I believe to be strengths, all that I can say that I know how to do, and about which I can rejoice in my own capacity. Before you start questioning my sanity, I invite you to evaluate the issue from the scriptures. Jesus says, "What is born from the flesh is flesh, and what is born from the Spirit is spirit"[12].

---

12 John 3:6 CJB.

Honestly, everything that we may be able to do in the flesh will only have fruits in the flesh. God can't accept anything from my worldly produce because that is the fruit of a fallen nature and derives from the decaying life we inherited from Adam. Therefore, no work produced by this nature will ever be considered good, but only what comes from the eternal life we inherited in Jesus.

Paul comes to this very conclusion and finally declares that all of his strength is useless and decides to rejoice in his weaknesses instead. He realised that all the strength from men is an illusion and transitory. If you and I think we're good at something, we're living with the focus on our own strength, which is limited and fleeting.

Until now, we have been talking about our weak points, but we need to wake up to the fact that even our strength is limited and even uselessly feeble before God. If our strength was useful, we could justify ourselves by our own acts; we could be found acceptable to God by what we do; then, with so many good attributes, who would need a saviour?

God, though, saw our incapacity, and he acted in our favour and provided salvation by His strength. If our strength was of any value, we could judge our brothers based on what we believe to be right or wrong, but since our weaknesses are just different to theirs, we're all equally dependent on God. Therefore, all man's strength is born of the flesh, of Adam's seed, and because of the corruption caused by sin, it is condemned to death and death on a cross.

If we live according to our strength, we will be living a lie because our strength is feeble and limited. You and I will often decide what to do solely based on our abilities. Thus, we only do what we think we know and don't do what we feel limited in.

Regarding God's calling, then, we will want to "decide" if God has called us to something or not based on our competence and our CV. In the same way, we decide not to engage in something when we consider ourselves incompetent at it.

While we do this, we are building walls around us, deeply founded in ourselves, our ideas, feelings or even based only on fear, which will prevent us from doing many things.

Unfortunately, we hardly question if the things we refrain from because of our limitations could be part of God's will for us. Similarly, we choose to engage in doing many things only because we feel qualified, without asking if that is the fulness of what God had planned. When we feel comfortable with our skills to do something, we just want to stay there, within our comfort zone, and we take consolation in the thought that "we're doing our part".

It's too easy to decide our paths by thinking: "I'm qualified for this, so that's what I'm going to do", or, "I don't know this, so it can't be my calling", or, "This I won't do, because I don't agree with it", or like we've already said before, "I'd rather die than speak in public". And just like that, we become the ones to create impediments and we become egocentric, not allowing God to move through us.

Finally, if we don't move because we don't feel adequate or move only on the things we feel qualified to do, we're only treading the path of our own knowledge in the flesh. If that's what we're doing, let's wake up, as we might be blocking the move of God.

Jesus said: "For the Spirit-Wind blows as it chooses. You can hear its sound, but you don't know where it came from or where it's going. So it is the same with those who are Spirit-born!"[13]. Those born again, Spirit-born, born of the very Spirit of God, should move according to this standard. The scripture says, "you hear its sound"; we must listen to the Holy Spirit and move when he moves.

So, when I use my limited human criteria to judge the situation and determine my direction, I'll be moving forward by myself and not by the Holy Spirit of God. While I continue making decisions like this, I'll be involuntarily fooling myself and reaching only the results according to my own strength. Alternatively, if I am

---

13 John 3:8 TPT.

grounded in the unlimited power of God, my results will also be equally limitless.

Some people think they have faith. They concentrate and put all the energy of their minds into believing in something. That is not faith, though. That is positive thinking. Because a faith that is produced in the flesh is flesh. But a faith produced by the Spirit of God, it is Spirit.

Some would say their faith is weak. Of course, it is. If the faith is ours, most certainly, it will be weak because if it's produced in the mind alone, the only fruit it will bear will be natural and not supernatural. What we produce in our mind (our humanity) is limited and will always bear limited and decaying fruits, but that which the Spirit of God produces is unlimited and bears fruits for eternity.

Some people would think that what's required to have a revival service is to turn up the volume while preaching, but a loud voice alone won't produce revival. The fruit of shouting is a hoarse voice (limited fruits). In contrast, if I hear the Lord and obey him, no matter whether I'm silent or shouting, the extraordinary results will come.

I've been in meetings where the power of God manifested powerfully through the life of a preacher with a dynamic voice, shouting and rejoicing. I've also been in meetings where the power of God manifested before the preacher had even moved from his place. The move of God does not depend on human ability.

Some may think they are better than others because of their abilities and strengths. Others may also think they are inferior to others because of their weaknesses. Some also think it's appropriate to "throw rocks" and apply judgements to others because they believe they are more righteous than them. However, if everyone knew that all the works produced in the flesh are weak and not strong, then nobody would consider himself superior. How liberating!

If anybody feels better than others and condemns and judges them, he's only demonstrating his fruits in the flesh. He's showing a life based only on weakness as if that could bear any "good fruit". Likewise, if anybody feels inferior to others, he's also showing a life according to the weakness of his own flesh.

If we live in the weakness of flesh we can only produce what the flesh can produce. Furthermore, all flesh is condemned to death because of the seed of Adam. However, what is lived in the Spirit of God will produce what God can produce: the extraordinary, the supernatural. The very life of God is manifested.

After all, why should I rejoice in my weakness?

Why should we rejoice? As we read previously: "But he said to me, 'My grace is sufficient for you, for my power is made perfect in weakness.' Therefore I will boast all the more gladly about my weaknesses, so that Christ's power may rest on me."[14].

Our weakness is a reason for great joy because without it we would not be able to see the power of God manifesting powerfully upon the Earth. The power of God can only manifest on us when we decide to be content that we are weak but still move ahead anyway. In other words, we need to stop trying to be strong!

The Lord's brave men and women are not the strong ones, but those who know they are weak! The Lord's brave ones are those who dare to do the impossible, even aware of their own complete incapacity, but confident in the power of God, for the glory of Jesus Christ.

The Lord's extraordinary will be experienced not by those trying to reach it by doing ordinary works. All human labour is ordinary; all we do as human beings is bound by the rules of this world. The extraordinary belongs to the Lord, and it will not happen as a result of

---

14 2 Corinthians 12:9.

human betterment. The extraordinary life is His life! The extraordinary faith is His faith! The extraordinary strength is His strength! He is extraordinary, and there's no way we can move extraordinarily without Him!

If there's sin, of course, we need to repent. His work on the cross ensures our forgiveness, reconciliation and redemption, but it's up to us to admit before him that we are weak. It's up to us to realise we cannot do it and rejoice instead of being sad about it.

It is up to us to recognise we can't even do the things we think we can. Then, we will be able to live in the power of God. Let us be honest before Him like the scripture says, "do not think of yourself more highly than you ought"[15]. Let us lay before him our weaknesses so that He may be powerful in us!

Recently, I was having a conversation with a pastor friend of mine about how central the Gospel of Jesus is; the message of the cross, the message of God's saving grace, and how all of us need the daily reminder of what the experience of salvation means.

I grew up in a Christian environment and have lived in a revival move of the Holy Spirit since very early in life. Yet, even then, the most crucial experience of my life was when I realised how weak and prone to failure I am, even to the point of becoming disillusioned with myself.

---

15 Romans 12:3.

In this place, God's grace reached out to me and brought me back up. The memory of that moment marks me like a precious scar that will never leave.

In anything I do, I am reminded of who I am as a natural being and how weak I am, but I am also reminded of how immense His grace is towards me to restore me back to His plan. This is my foundation, the memory of the work of the cross in me. Under its authority, I move; with its strength, I walk. I can't depend on myself for anything, but the Holy Spirit in me can do all things.

You and I need these precious scars. We need this consciousness. We need to bring the work on that cross to mind every day of our lives, lay down our hearts to Him, and say: "Lord, I am weak; here's my weakness. Be strong in me! Live in me! Move through me!".

Get out of your hiding place

The irony is that you and I spend our lives thinking that to be used by God, we need to be perfect and that all of the people we've heard stories about were also perfect, while in reality, nobody is and nobody ever was. God decides to work with the imperfect, the flawed and the weak. The weakness is the prerequisite for the power of God to operate.

The power of God manifests in its fullness and perfection in our weakness. But how can His power manifest in us if we hide and don't acknowledge our weaknesses? God teaches us that we should not use the criteria of our experience and knowledge to decide on which steps to take and which works to do. Indeed, we need to consider the experience and knowledge of the one who is higher than us, the Almighty.

Our greatest opportunities to see God in action will be when we are doing the things we consider ourselves to be weak at. Furthermore, if we decide to regard even our strengths as weaknesses, we will also see the power of God manifesting in its fullness.

The world says, "Being weak is an embarrassment" but, God says, "Recognising weakness is indispensable". The world says, "Hide all your weaknesses" but God says: "Confess them before me". The world says, "Be sad about your weaknesses" but the Lord says, "My joy is your strength". The world says, "Do not go further than this point" but the Lord says to you as he said once to Peter, "Come". Peter, then, got out of the boat and stepped firmly upon the waters of the storm[16].

When I do what I know, I could "boast on that", using Paul's words: I could rejoice in the things I know. I would

---

16 " 'Come,' he said. Then Peter got down out of the boat, walked on the water and came towards Jesus. ", Mathew 14:29.

be inclined to consider myself higher than others while "boasting" in myself, in my own knowledge and skills.

The apostle Paul experienced the power of God manifesting so much in his weakness that he decided even his strength was not strong enough. He desired to see the power of God moving in the same way in all areas of his life.

The enemy wants to imprison you, persuading you to think you can only do anything for God if you are sufficiently competent, educated, and qualified. The Bible, though, is teaching us, in Paul's words, that when I am capable and strong, the power of God cannot manifest in its fullness. It's only when I don't know and am sure I'm not able that the power of God will be made perfect upon me.

If I refuse to do something because I think I'm not good enough, that's the equivalent of declaring that God doesn't have the power to do that in me. Also, if I do something because I think I'm good at that, it's like declaring that I don't need the power of God to operate in me.

My family, for example, has been very much connected to music for as long as I can remember. Musical talent is something that's present in all of us. Since my childhood, we all got involved with learning musical instruments and singing and my brothers have truly extraordinary musical skills. For me, it would be very comfortable to think that my service for the Lord is only music-related because of this natural ability.

Even with the best intentions, my natural inclination would be my limitation. My lack of eloquence and introverted personality would determine that I should never participate in other activities like preaching God's Word or even evangelisation.

Against my natural skills and inclination, God surprised me by calling me to lead an evangelistic ministry, which I did for many years alongside the beloved brethren in the cities of Ponta Grossa and Carambeí[17]. Yet, even in that position, while guiding and training people for that mission, I always thought of myself as naturally unsuitable for the role.

However, when I stepped out and made myself available to obey God's voice, I marvelled daily at the fruits, with an absolute conviction that they were not because of me since all I was doing was coming from a position of weakness. The weakness, then, was leading me to a place of much greater dependency on God.

This same conviction became the heart of everyone engaged in that ministry. Other people who had previously been hiding in their comfort zone started to step out and listen to the voice of God too. As a result, a unique movement of God happened over that time.

---

17 TN: Ponta Grossa and Carambeí are cities in the state of Parana, in Brazil.

All our congregation was being stirred into a deeper pursuit of God's presence. The Church was going out of its four walls to visit hospitals, care homes, prisons, and many other social and evangelistic projects that impacted whole neighbourhoods. Once we took a step forward and started to experience the power of God moving through all of us, we all shared an indescribable joy in our souls, which marked us deeply.

It would have been a lot easier if I had just stayed in my comfort zone, but what I experienced and learned from God in those days cannot be matched. Think about it: If I only move when I think I'm good enough, in whose strength am I moving?

If I only do what I know, I do everything by my strength. But if I dare to do what I don't know when God is leading me to it, surely I can only trust in His strength because I know how much I really can't.

If I only do what I know, where is my faith? Doesn't that make my faith null and carnal? But if I make myself available to do even what I don't know, I'm expressing my faith with deeds. So then, my faith is genuine and spiritual.

Nothing can, and nothing shall stop us! Therefore, if I remove myself from the equation, moving or not must be exclusively based on what God can or cannot do.

Now think about this: What is impossible for God? Is there anything God can't do? We have been called for freedom, and freedom is in Jesus Christ. Being free is living according to His life, doing what He can do, moving where He can move, and speaking whenever He speaks.

You and I need to get out of our hiding places. You and I need to stop and reconsider our comfort zone and weaknesses. Finally, you and I need to believe with the faith of God. If our weakness is a lack of faith, we need to ask Him to be strong for us in faith. If our weakness is an addiction, we need to ask Him to be the strength we need to overcome it. If our weaknesses are sins, we need Him to be the remission and victory on us. If our weakness is in the way we speak, we need to allow Him to speak through us!

David said: "The Lord is the strength of my life; of whom shall I be afraid?"[18]. Throughout biblical history and through Church history, we see weak and improbable people doing extraordinary things by the power of the Holy Spirit of God; that happens time after time. We could talk about Abraham, Noah, Joseph, Moses, David or Gideon, among many others.

Let's go back to the story of the prophet Jonah and how he intended to flee from the presence of God to avoid doing the mission presented to him. Many have

---

18 Psalms 27:1a NKJV.

studied the book and many theories have been made about the reasons behind Jonah's flight.

We could speculate that Jonah didn't agree with his mission, or maybe he didn't feel adequate or prepared for it. Perhaps Jonah didn't believe the Assyrians were worthy of the message. Another theory is that Jonah was worried about his reputation and didn't want to prophesy about an event of destruction that likely wouldn't happen.

Whatever his motivations were, Jonah's weaknesses were based on the boundaries and constraints of his own soul. All his possible justifications were self-centred, based on the things he was or was not able to do, or the things he wanted and didn't want to do; Jonah's will was his greatest limitation.

Jonah went as far as losing his own life to save his will. When he got to the very bottom, having been three days already in the fish's belly, or symbolically in the womb of death, Jonah is included back in God's plan and is called again to perform his mission.

God was not surprised by Jonah's weaknesses, and despite them, God decided to include Jonah again in His plan. Jonah went ahead, then, and supernaturally travelled a path that should have taken three days in only one. His mission not only took place but it was an absolute success and delivered extraordinary results.

The one who was not up to the mission, the one none of us would have chosen to perform the task was the one

God chose. The work accomplished there was certainly not achieved in any human strength. Jonah shouldn't even have been physically alive but symbolically returns from the dead to proclaim the message to that city. The work done through God, by the unreliable Jonah, was extraordinary, and a whole town found a place for repentance and salvation from their terrible fate.

Jesus himself declared: "without Me you can do nothing"[19]. Understanding this truth is simply liberating. Knowing that God uses us and includes us in his plans despite ourselves is just amazing.

Therefore, my prayer is that we may thank God for our weaknesses, rejoice in them, and find even more joy because He is the strength in us. May we all live with boldness in the power of God, based on His strength and not on ours. May we move today based on what He says about us and on what His word establishes. He is our trust! He is our glory! He is our strength!

---

19 "I am the vine, you are the branches. He who abides in Me, and I in him, bears much fruit; for without Me you can do nothing.", John 15:5 NKJV.

WEARINESS AND OVERLOAD

I have many precious memories from my childhood and youth, and I'm really grateful for them. In many aspects, however, my childhood wasn't exactly straightforward. I can honestly say that everything I've done in life has been with a lot of effort. I don't remember having any special privileges for anything, but I had to work hard and study a great deal to progress in every step of my life.

Since my teens, I had to work with my parents in our family business, a bakery. In between many batches of bread and many delivery trips, I learned the values of work and effort. These are treasures I carry with me to this day.

In the same way that I learned these values, very early on I got to know the other side of what comes with hard work. No matter what kind of work it is, it will always be accompanied by tiredness.

I remember a time I was helping my dad take a delivery to a small neighbourhood shop, and a calendar fixed to the wall behind the cashier got my attention. It had a drawing of a man lying down under a tree by a river. The man was resting, very relaxed, with his hands behind his head, and a contented expression on his face. He was dressed like a countryman, unshaven, with a straw hat to cover his eyes and he was chewing on a small piece of grass. The calendar had a label underneath, saying: "Do you know what I do when I'm tired of doing nothing? I rest…"

Jokes aside, tiredness is a given with any work, no matter what kind. Maybe somebody might get tired of doing nothing, but for sure, tiredness is normal and expected when one works. Tiredness doesn't come as a surprise because it is, by definition, the weariness that comes every time we do an activity continuously.

I'm confident we can all remember many situations when we've been tired or even downright exhausted. The bakery, for example, introduced me to the concept of working long hours since my youth. Later, while working as a software developer, I had my fair share of working through nights and weekends.

For the last few years, I've suffered daily on public transport commuting to work every day with all the other Londoners. Although we've been talking about many types of physical tiredness, maybe the most extreme seasons for me were those where I've felt drained of strength in my soul.

I've been through many of these moments throughout my life, where it would seem I got to the end of the road, with no hope ahead of me. Some years ago, for example, when my daughter Louise was just one year old, I got a job offer from a huge company. If I accepted, it would mean moving to Dublin in Ireland. The company would be covering all relocation costs, sponsoring for visas and everything else. So naturally, my wife and I got really excited. It was a dream come true.

With the signed contract in my hands, I left my job, disposed of all our things, handed over the flat, and all we had left in life was crammed into four suitcases. We went to stay at my parents' in Ponta Grossa[20] while waiting for the work permit. The two weeks of waiting passed, and then we got a negative response; our work permit was not approved. The company then appealed to

20 TN: A city in the state of Parana, in Brazil.

the government, which extended the wait for yet another four months, only to get a final negative response.

I have no words to describe the anguish of those days of waiting and the frustration that that negative response had brought. Our dreams and expectations were falling apart and worse, there was the embarrassment of meeting people again and explaining to them what had happened. Each time we had to relive the pain.

We couldn't see an inch in front of our faces. It looked like we were headed on a path of ruin and our dreams could never come true. We didn't know, though, what was about to happen. This crisis was leading us to seek God's face with more intensity. It led us to understand that He was about to do something, and it was necessary for us to stay in Brazil a little longer, or even more specifically, in Ponta Grossa.

The time we stayed there was essential for our lives. There, we learned to depend on God. He sustained us, and we found our true vocation and calling. We served the Church and the people of that city, evangelised, fed the hungry, visited prisons and hospitals, saw miracles, saw salvation, trained others and collaborated with God to awaken callings and ministries. In that place, we also received a precious gift in the revelation of God's word, special food that sustained us for many years and throughout many hardships, so that we would become able to share a part of it with you now.

While I was experiencing extreme exhaustion of my soul in those early days, I couldn't see where God was taking things. Now I can see God's grace in everything that happened to us. I also discovered how highly debilitating weariness of the soul is.

Paul goes one step further when he writes: "never tire of doing what is good"[21], which means it's possible even to get tired of doing what is good. This kind of tiredness can, indeed, present itself as the ultimate impediment to the purposes of God in our lives. If we want to keep doing what's good, we need to learn how to deal with it.

We can see examples of people who found themselves weary and exhausted in their souls throughout the Bible. For me, one of the most outstanding is when the prophet Elijah, having defeated the prophets of Baal, feared for his life and ran away to the desert. Completely exhausted, he took refuge in the shadow of a tree. Elijah had reached his limit. He prayed to God, asking to die, and then slept. God didn't judge him but instead helped him to recover. An angel of the Lord woke him up and gave him bread to eat and that meal sustained him for

---

21 2 Thessalonians 3:13.

an extraordinary journey in which Elijah ran for forty days and forty nights[22].

And, of course, another example would be Jonah, the prophet. His soul was against the calling and purpose of God and led him on a course of ruin and death. I don't think his decision to go in the wrong direction was easy, but while the scripture doesn't go into much detail, Jonah must have experienced significant internal conflict. Inwardly, he might have even given up fighting when he said, "throw me into the sea"[23], to be eaten by that enormous fish[24]. Then, in the belly of death, Jonah saw a great light and rose again to fulfil what God had called him to do.

---

22 "Elijah was afraid and ran for his life. When he came to Beersheba in Judah, he left his servant there, while he himself went a day's journey into the wilderness. He came to a broom bush, sat down under it and prayed that he might die. 'I have had enough, Lord,' he said. 'Take my life; I am no better than my ancestors.' Then he lay down under the bush and fell asleep. All at once an angel touched him and said, 'Get up and eat.' He looked around, and there by his head was some bread baked over hot coals, and a jar of water. He ate and drank and then lay down again. The angel of the Lord came back a second time and touched him and said, 'Get up and eat, for the journey is too much for you.' So he got up and ate and drank. Strengthened by that food, he travelled for forty days and forty nights until he reached Horeb, the mountain of God." 1 Kings 19:3-8.

23 Jonah 1:12.

24 Jonah 1:17.

Jesus acknowledges tiredness when he extends the invitation: "Come to Me, all you who are weary and burdened, and I will give you rest. Take My yoke upon you and learn from Me; for I am gentle and humble in heart, and you will find rest for your souls. For My yoke is easy and My burden is light"[25].

Note that apart from weariness, Jesus also talks about being burdened. They may seem the same thing, but, in reality, they are not. The distinction Jesus makes here is not an accident or coincidence, but we might need to dig a little deeper to work out what he meant.

The majority of the New Testament was written in Greek, as we know, as that was the commercial and cultural language back then. So, if we look at original manuscripts, we will find the word *"kopiaó"*, which translates into "weariness". This word means labouring until wearing out and becoming completely exhausted. It has its roots in another Greek word, *"kópos"*, which may indicate somebody being hit by a very intense blow or something that debilitates and weakens severely; it means a very extreme and weakening fatigue.

Then, if we look for the other Greek word, which translates into "burdened", we will find *"pephortismenoi"*. Its more literal translation indicates a non-transferable load or burden that is so heavy that it causes a person to bend, its load preventing them from standing straight.

Weariness comes from excessive labour, the repetitive and continuous exposure to work. If somebody usually runs six miles every day, he will get to the end of this training tired. But if he runs twelve miles that day he will be exhausted.

Being burdened or overloaded differs from weariness because it comes from extreme exposure, causing the person to bend over, even preventing them from standing. If we continue with the same example, a runner that usually runs six miles will not be able to run a full marathon of twenty-six miles, they would certainly faint halfway through it.

What would happen when we use an electric appliance, like a vacuum cleaner, and we leave it on for a very long time? It would heat up. Exposure to this kind of stress alone can damage the device. ThIs is the same as weariness. Now, suppose we take an electric appliance designed for Europe, for a 110 volts current, and use it in the United Kingdom, where the electric current is 220 volts. In this case, the device will suffer an overload that would cause all its internal components to be damaged. This is the same as the overload we're talking about.

Similarly, mechanical scales will not stand a weight heavier than what they are designed to. If the scales we have in our homes can weigh items up to twenty stone, what would happen if a weight of thirty stone was put on them? The internal components would not handle the pressure, and they would break.

What would happen to the vacuum cleaner or scales after they had been exposed to a limit beyond what they could handle? They would become useless and ultimately lose their purpose. They would, in the end, have to be thrown away, as they would be good for nothing anymore.

In the context of the verses we've read, Jesus also talks about extreme exposure. He is talking about an extreme form of tiredness and of carrying weights that are way too heavy, so heavy that the person carrying them bends and is not able to stand again. Jesus is talking about a scenario where the risk of utter destruction and uselessness is imminent.

It's interesting to note that Jesus is not talking about a generic kind of weariness and overload here, but one particular type.

The weariness and the overload of the soul

Jesus declares: "and you will find rest for your souls". When Jesus talks about rest, he's not talking about a general type of weariness but the specific weariness and overload of the soul. This scriptural truth is a lot deeper than it seems at first.

So that we can understand what that means for you and me, I would like to go back to what the scripture teaches about the human soul. The Bible says that we are formed by three distinct elements: spirit, soul and body.

The part of ourselves called "spirit", receives the life that comes from the Holy Spirit when we believe for salvation. The Spirit of God gives life to our spirit, which is otherwise dead or inactive. In the spirit we have fellowship and a relationship with Him. From the spirit, all God's power flows into and from our lives.

Our spirit is the most important part of us, because our eternal life depends on it. The purpose of the spirit is to be a fountain of living waters within that will both satisfy us and quench the thirst of others. It's up to us, though, whether we receive this salvation by God's grace and allow our spirit to be revived.

We can become depleted of strength and cause un-pleasant consequences to our bodies if we go beyond our limits or if we do things we weren't intended to do. For example, some people can run entire marathons, while others might get serious health consequences by running a distance of just a little more than one block.

If we strain ourselves until exhaustion we will feel exhausted. If we want to carry a weight heavier than what we're able to, we'll feel overwhelmed in our bodies, and we won't be able to carry out the activity to its completion. Even if everyone's personal limits are different, going beyond them will have the same consequences. We can also cause weariness and an overload in our souls if we operate in a way that we weren't intended to. For example, suppose you and I use our souls incorrectly and put too much pressure on them? They might even collapse and leave us useless, so it's vital that we learn about the purpose and limits of our souls, so we don't lose our own lives.

When we look at the original manuscripts, in Greek, the word translated as "soul" is the word *"psychais"*. This same word can also translate as "life". The soul is the part of us that includes our will, emotions and intellect. It's our rational, intellectual and emotional being; it's where our motivation and decisions come from.

So, what exactly is the cause of tiredness and overload of the soul? What are the things that take us to the point of exhaustion? The root of tiredness and overload in the soul is using it outside of its original purpose. If we expose our souls to too much stress, it could take us to extreme exhaustion; we might find ourselves knocked out, dismayed, and even completely lose the very purpose of our existence.

We really need to be aware of how important this is. Our very life depends on it. God's projects for us depend on us staying alive, active, awakened, and motivated, but if we let our souls take on a different role from the one designed by God, we risk losing everything.

At the same time, however, we see God's grace expressed sovereignly in the words of Jesus. We see Jesus offering a solution even to those already in a state of exhaustion and uselessness. It's never too late for us to come to Him and find rest for our souls.

The yoke from Jesus

If we turn our attention to the words of Jesus: "Take my yoke upon you and learn from me, for I am gentle and humble in heart, and you will find rest for your souls. For my yoke is easy and my burden is light", we see that He is calling for everyone who is weary or overloaded to come and take His yoke.

I used to be a little confused about this. Why would Jesus use an illustration like this to talk about rest? A yoke was a big piece of wood that was placed over two animals, like oxen, or donkeys, to align them together in the direction they were supposed to go. This traditional agricultural practice was necessary when preparing a field for planting.

The animals were set together, side by side, and the yoke placed on their necks. Then, the plough was connected to it. The animals would go forward in a line, pulling the plough, which would produce furrows in the ground. The seeds would then be sowed in those furrows.

I started to ask myself, what would be the relationship between the rest of the soul and this agricultural activity? What was in God's mind when He made this comparison? What is the role of the yoke and its importance in this context? What difference would that yoke make for the ox involved in that sowing activity?

To find answers to these questions, we need to think about what would happen to the ox if it were left without the yoke. Let's imagine that we wanted to prepare a field for planting, so instead of putting the yoke upon the ox, we only put the plough behind it. If we then "gave instructions" to the ox, saying that it needed to walk in a straight line because the field needs to have several parallel lines, what would happen?

The ox would not be able to understand our instructions. The nature of the ox would lead him to wander and not in a straight line, but it would walk towards food and water. Ultimately, the ox would instinctively seek to satisfy its own needs. Nothing that it would do in that field could ever be useful for agriculture. If we could look at the pictures of that field on Google Maps, later, we would see a bunch of squiggly lines. At the end of the day, the ox would not have accomplished any of the its owners' projects, its nature would have simply assured him a full stomach.

That animal's instinctive and limited mind would lead him to seek only its own comfort and satiety. So all the strength of the ox, all its potential, would only be used according to what his limited mind could visualise, and it would be limited to satisfying itself.

The yoke could, at first, look like a source of oppression, imposing alignment and limitations. It would not allow the ox to "just follow its heart" or its stomach. Therefore, while equipped with that yoke, when coming to the end of that day of work, that ox would have accomplished something far beyond the potential of its own intellect. The animal would not have been able to understand the plan to plant the field but while subject to the yoke, it became a participant in the man's projects.

The ox alone, without that yoke, could never plough a field. The ox, by itself, would only manage to fill his stomach, but all of that would be void of purpose. That is, it would have turned his purpose vain or useless. So what would seem like a limiter to the ox was, in reality, what increased its potential to do extraordinary works, far beyond what it could imagine.

The ox's strength was channelled into a purpose that was higher than itself. Indeed, God designed the ox to be strong and serve the man with his physical strength. However, for that ox to be useful to man, and for the purposes of the man to be fulfilled in the ox's life, a yoke needed to be placed over that ox.

Now, using this parable, Jesus' analogy starts to make more sense. Weariness and overload in the soul are caused by utilising our souls in a way disconnected from the original design established by God. Jesus brings us back to the original design and invites us to take His yoke. Operating without the yoke of Jesus corrupts, destroys and brings our souls to exhaustion.

So, what we thought was a limitation is actually the very thing that helps us accomplish extraordinary things. The overload in our soul is, in fact, the lack of the yoke and not its presence. The overload of the soul happens in the absence of alignment, limits, direction, counsel, and wisdom from the Holy Spirit of God in our lives.

If we limit and align ourselves, focussed on a straight path, a fit purpose and in the right direction, our soul will exert itself beyond its limits. If our soul lacks direction, it tends to choose the way it wants. So if we follow the purposes of our own heart and obey the will of our soul, we won't accomplish anything and will only walk in circles.

What we recognise in our culture as freedom doesn't bring any comfort for a man's heart. Following our heart is not only the source of human distress, it's also the source of weariness and overload. God has designed our soul to live under the will and guidance of the Holy

Spirit; our soul has not been designed to give direction to our lives.

Once, while sharing with friends about these things, I talked about an experience that each one of us had already had, one way or the other. The name of this experience is the "lazy day". A lazy day is when you have no work or school, so you wake up late. Everything you want to do that day is reduced to entertainment and food. You watch Netflix, play video games, eat popcorn, eat sweets[26], eat hot dogs, and finally rent a movie and order a pizza.

Have you had a day like this? I find it funny that when you come to the end of the day, after spending the whole day doing only what you want, you are more tired than when you started.

If the will of our souls produced rest, shouldn't I come to the end of that day with even greater motivation to work, conquer and triumph? Conversely, it seems that the more I do my own will, the more I "follow my heart" or satisfy the wishes of my soul, the more tired I get.

---

26 NT: The original says "brigadeiro", a traditional sweet from Brazil, like a chewy chocolate truffle.

Our heart is perverse, evil, selfish, and will always seek to do its own will. "The heart is deceitful above all things, and desperately wicked; who can know it?"[27]

The opposite is also true. Maybe you have also looked at your calendar in the morning, to everything you had to do, and there were simply too many things, too much work to do. Now, in God, if you decide to launch yourself into the work ahead of you, you go out there and conquer, triumph, and reach the end of that day, surprised by how many things you managed to accomplish.

If you have watched the movie Wall-E, from Pixar, you'll recognise a clear example of this. Beyond the cute and funny romance between the garbage recycler robot, Wall-E, and the explorer robot, Eva, the story is fascinating.

The movie happens in a not very distant future, in which humanity is forced out of Earth. The planet cannot produce life anymore because of the excessive amount of garbage. Mankind deals with the problem by building giant spaceships to send people to space to search for a new home. However, part of their mission is to constantly observe the home planet, in the hope that it will start producing life again.

---

27 Jeremiah 17:9 NKJV.

Since the ships offer every possible luxury and comfort, people don't even get up from their chairs, they float around. Generations pass, and humanity becomes even lazier, and everything they do revolves around entertainment and food. They become sedentary and only interested in satisfying themselves. The most interesting thing is that not one of them can even remember their original mission.

While living the utopia of having all of their wishes satisfied, they lost the mission's focus and the purpose of their very existence. While this was a work of fiction, I think we can learn from it as a parable.

As we've seen before, scripture teaches us that if we hand over the direction of our lives to ourselves and guide our steps using our own will, our destiny will be exhaustion and depletion.

Taking the yoke from Jesus

Jesus teaches us: "So do not worry, saying, 'What shall we eat?' or 'What shall we drink?' or 'What shall we wear?' For the pagans run after all these things, and your heavenly Father knows that you need them. But seek first his kingdom and his righteousness, and all these things will be given to you as well. Therefore do not worry about tomorrow, for tomorrow will worry about itself. Each day has enough trouble of its own."[28].

The original design from God for our souls did not include worrying about such things. Our heart was not made to focus on what to eat or wear. Our soul was not made to carry this burden. Another translation says: "for it is the pagans who set their hearts on all these things". The pagans set their hearts, souls, will and all their energy pursuing these things. But we, who belong to God and are born again, restored and called to "Life", don't. God restores us to the original design. We have someone who looks after us.

However, our heart and soul must be subject to God's will, to His Kingdom and Justice. If our heart is subject to God's will, to His Kingdom and Justice, all those things will be given to us. God's original design for our souls is for us to be under the yoke of Christ, subject to Him and walking alongside Him. If we hand over the direction of our lives to our souls, there will only be frustration, dissatisfaction, weariness and overload.

Jesus' focus with this teaching is for us to set our hearts in the right place and to bring us back into the ideal position that God prepared for us. Being subject to His yoke is not a limitation, but the one thing that opens doors and launches us into our greatest potential.

---

28 Matthew 6:31-34.

To pursue all those things, and follow our own will, will certainly cause depletion, distress, fear, sadness and anguish. It's enough to look at the world around us to realise that this pursuit is just not worth it. Jesus teaches us, saying, "For what will it profit a man if he gains the whole world, and loses his own soul?"[29]

God did not design our souls to live this way. If we do it, we will undoubtedly get completely exhausted, and because of the overload, we will eventually become useless. Our soul was made to submit to our spirit and the Holy Spirit of God. He is the one to give purpose, direction and potential to our lives.

Decisions regarding which path to follow can be stressful. Should I turn left or right? Should I live in my country or abroad? Should I take a job at this company or another? Should I choose agriculture or engineering? Questions about our path are a source of constant concern, and they are frequently a cause for depression, knocking us down and causing us to be knocked back and overloaded.

Inspired by the Holy Spirit, Jeremiah wrote: "Lord, I know that people's lives are not their own; it is not for them to direct their steps."[30]. In a different translation, we read: "Adonai, I know that the way of humans is not

29 Mark 8:36 NKJV.

30 Jeremiah 10:23.

in their control, humans are not able to direct their steps as they walk."[31].

Mankind was not made to lead its own way. The human intellect, emotions and will are not the basis for our decision making. As the scripture says, the way of humans is not in their control, and they cannot direct their steps as they walk.

The human life, heart and soul, are not made to choose their own steps; this is the responsibility of the Lord, our God. When operating outside of the purpose for which it was created, the human soul will find weariness, overload, hopelessness, sadness, and pain. But if the human soul is under the direction of the Holy Spirit of God, it will find a higher purpose and extraordinary strength.

"Then Jesus said to His disciples, "If anyone desires to come after Me, let him deny himself, and take up his cross, and follow Me. For whoever desires to save his life will lose it, but whoever loses his life for My sake will find it. For what profit is it to a man if he gains the whole world, and loses his own soul? Or what will a man give in exchange for his soul?"[32]

Jesus says that we will find rest for our souls, but doing what our soul wants, without the alignment from

---

31 Jeremiah 10:23 CJB.

32 Matthew 16:24-26 NKJV.

God, without His yoke, will only produce overload and weariness. It's not the limitation that oppresses us, but the lack of it. It's not being led that oppresses us, but the lack of direction. A weary soul is an unsubmissive one, not yet governed by the Holy Spirit of God. It carries the burden of living according to itself. The weary soul is the one without the yoke of Jesus. The rest Jesus offers for our souls consists of placing a yoke upon them, which gives alignment, correction and focus, and it is easy and light.

When we talk about our souls, I believe many of us will tend only to consider our emotions and our will, but let's not forget that our soul also includes our intellect. The reasoning and the logic are also part of the soul. So, just like we should not put our emotions and our will in control of our lives, our intellect should not take that position either.

When we seek to go deeper into God's truth, there's a considerable risk of falling into the trap of thinking about God's words in the same way we do about philosophies and human thoughts. Many of us have adhered to schools of thought and, in favour of defending our own ideas, have caused division in the Lord's Church. Human thoughts and points of view are of minimal value because they originate from human weakness. Indeed, real value comes only from the life that comes from the Holy Spirit of God.

With every good intention, we might zealously end up defending philosophies, religions, theologies, rules and rites, or even getting into debates and endless discussions. For generations, we have fooled ourselves and created silos of our own Christian groups, ignoring the reality of the Body of Christ as it is: one. As a result, we put ourselves at the risk of thinking we need to be "super believers", seeing ourselves as the Avengers[33] of Christianity, defending a human betterment that denies the very work of the Cross.

The Cross has "sinful humanity" at its starting point and the futility of every effort towards goodness. The Cross represents God himself provisioning the payment of the debt of all of us, transporting us into the status of justified and holy. It is God accomplishing what was once impossible for us. The Cross gives us access to the very life of God by the Holy Spirit, without which we can't overcome anything. The Cross is not our beginning, but our every day, because we will keep on being weak and, without Him, it is impossible for us to overcome or accomplish anything good.

When we look to ourselves and face our weaknesses, and we do that daily, we are again taking up the Cross. "Then he said to them all: 'Whoever wants to be my disciple must deny themselves and take up their cross

---

33 *The Avengers*™ is a trademark of Marvel Characters, Inc.

daily and follow me."[34] So our human efforts cannot produce anything good. It's only by the power of God through the Holy Spirit that we're actually able to align our souls to wanting to do something good. In other words, the transformation of our lives is not a pre-condition for us to be able to access heavenly realities, but the consequence of what He does for us and of a daily relationship of dependence on God, by the power of his Holy Spirit.

If we lose our time and effort focusing on personal improvement, we could inadvertently be placing stones in our own path and other people's paths. We would only be multiplying frustration, tiredness and overload when our intention was precisely the opposite. While zealously pursuing one thing, we might end up obtaining the opposite result, amplifying the glory of men, diminishing the Glory of God and almost nullifying the Cross.

The fruits of these kinds of efforts will be division, confusion, disputes, stress, lack of focus and, often, will cause the little ones to get lost along the way.

It is with great fear of God that I write these words. I believe it's time for the Church to come back to the centrality of Christ, the integrity of the Gospel and the unity in the Spirit. It's time for us to find rest for our

---

34 Luke 9:23.

souls, take the yoke from Jesus, and let the Holy Spirit of God govern our lives.

And Jesus goes further, saying, "and learn of me, for I am meek and humble of heart, and ye shall find rest for your souls."[35]. What does it mean to be meek and humble of heart? What is this attitude that Christ had?

Paul explains it in his letter to the Philippians: "In your relationships with one another, have the same mindset as Christ Jesus: who, being in very nature God, did not consider equality with God something to be used to his own advantage; rather, he made himself nothing by taking the very nature of a servant, being made in human likeness. And being found in appearance as a man, he humbled himself by becoming obedient to death – even death on a cross!"[36].

Jesus was meek and humble of heart. The verses we read speak about us having the same mindset: the same attitude of soul and of heart that Jesus had. He emptied himself and assumed the very nature of a servant.

If we continue with our parable, we can observe that there was also an animal that represented the figure of a servant in Jewish culture. More than any other, this animal was the donkey. And Jesus, coming as a servant,

---

35 Matthew 11:29 JUB.

36 Philippians 2:5-8.

humbled himself and entered Jerusalem mounted on one[37].

It's very poetic for us to say: "let us submit our souls to the Spirit of God". But that, in practical terms, means to say no to ourselves and take on the very nature of a servant, just like Jesus did. A servant does not do what he wants but the will of the one he serves.

In the Old Testament, we find a verse that says: "Do not plough with an ox and a donkey yoked together."[38]. A yoke was not something one animal could use alone, but it had places for two animals that should walk together. But from this scripture, we understand that the ox, which we established already is a strong animal, should not be put together with a donkey, a servant animal.

While left to our passions and desires, we could be compared to a wild ox, whose purpose is completely lost and under-utilised. Jesus, however, took the nature of a servant and decided to surrender his soul to the Holy Spirit of God. For this reason, we should have never been invited to participate in the same yoke as Jesus.

We didn't deserve the invitation to take on the same yoke as Jesus; an ox and a donkey should never be together under the same yoke. Jesus, though, makes the invitation. What impresses me the most is the order he

---

37 Matthew 21:7.

38 Deuteronomy 22:10.

establishes. Jesus doesn't demand that we first become like a servant, and only then can we be accepted under his yoke, in his rest. No. First, Jesus says, "Take my yoke", and then he says, "learn of me, for I am meek and humble of heart". So, first, Jesus extends rest to us; and then he volunteers to teach us to walk with him in this path.

That is, for me, one of the most impressive demonstrations of the love and the grace of God. Jesus understands the human condition. Jesus comprehends that, without this yoke, we will never be able to find our true purpose and the meaning for our existence. Jesus understands we need the Holy Spirit of God to overcome the challenges and concerns of this life and He invites us to share the victory He already established himself. Jesus invites us to live the extraordinary with him.

Passing to power

The prophet Isaiah, inspired by the Holy Spirit, writes, "He gives power to the weak, and to those who have no might He increases strength. Even the youths shall faint and be weary, and the young men shall utterly fall, but those who wait on the Lord shall renew their strength; they shall mount up with wings like eagles, they shall run and not be weary, they shall walk and not faint."[39].

I've read these verses many times, but with the wrong perspective, and I believe the mistake I was making while reading this scripture might also be the same mistake many of us make. Here, we think the word "wait" talks about time, as if it referred to a chronological time of waiting. The word wait, in this context, indicates "expectancy" or even "hope".

The scripture is telling us that those who wait and put their expectation, hope and dependency on the Lord will have their strength increased. The words of Jesus echo together with the words of the prophet Isaiah. They are declaring rest and renewal for those who come to Him.

The word "increases" was the translator's choice, but, in the original manuscripts, it comes with a connotation of exchange, of replacement. There's another version of the Bible in the English language, called *Young's Literal Translation*, which aims for the most literal possible expressions while looking at the original text.

Reading from this version[40], this passage from Isaiah looks like this: "He is giving power to the weary, And to

---

39 Isaiah 40:29-31 NKJV.

40 NT: In the original, this section differs slightly as the author has made his own translation of this passage, while the original text from YLT98 is used here.

those not strong He increaseth might. Even youths are wearied and fatigued, And young men utterly stumble, But those *expecting* Jehovah *pass [to] power*, They raise up the pinion as eagles, They run and are not fatigued, They go on and do not faint!"[41].

If we look for examples in the scripture, we will find many, but I think it's once again relevant to mention Jonah, the prophet. He was also an example of someone who let his soul lead him to destruction. In opposing God's orders, Jonah did all he could to take control of his steps.

The Bible tells us how Jonah went down to Joppa, went down into the ship, then down to the sea, and was finally thrown into the waters, going down once again. After having been swallowed by the fish, he descended one last time, now to the very roots of the mountains. All these references to descents are not there by chance. Jonah found himself in the lowest of the low places. Some commentators even say Jonah actually died because, in some parts of his prayer, he says "my soul" instead of saying "I".

Anyway, Jonah was at the lowest place of his life, exhausted and destroyed by the will of his soul. When he surrendered the lead to God, Jonah passed from weakness into power, or even from death to life. The resurrection

---

41 Isaiah 40:29-31 YLT98.

power is then typified in Jonah, the same power that resurrected our Lord Jesus Christ and now lives in us. When he passed to power, Jonah's potential multiplied, and he accomplished an extraordinary mission, higher than anything he could ever have reached by himself.

Those whose expectations are in the Lord, who set their hope in Him, will exchange tiredness with power. They pass from weakness to power. They are transported from a reality of frailty into a reality of power. They are transported from their minimal and limited strength into a tremendous potential in His power. Their potential multiplies, and extraordinary things can happen. This passage of the scripture carries on saying, "They will soar on wings like eagles"[42]; this declaration, by itself, is already talking about something impossible, supernatural.

If we set our expectancy in Him and place ourselves under this yoke from Jesus, if we align our expectations, put our hope in the right place and allow our soul to be guided by Him, we will start experiencing the extraordinary. If measured only according to ourselves, our potential will be minimal. But, if we decide to place our soul in the correct position, under this yoke from the Lord, and set our expectations on Him, our true potential will come to life.

---

42 Isaiah 40:31.

From this moment on, the one who was once weary and overloaded, when passing to power, accesses a new spiritual reality in which he can fly like an eagle and run without ever getting tired.

The Bible doesn't tell us we won't have problems. On the contrary, those who made history with God lived through countless hardships. So what have they done to overcome, and even extraordinarily, while still struggling in their souls? One thing, they transferred their expectancy to the Lord. Then, as they passed to power, they accessed the extraordinary life.

My prayer is that you and I won't allow weariness and overload to stop us. May we wake up today into the reality of our potential. May we position our lives under the yoke of the Lord and allow ourselves to be guided by Him. May we set our expectancy in Him to be transported from weakness into power. Let us lay aside the weariness and access this new tremendous spiritual reality, in which we will run without ever getting weary.

FEELING DEFEATED

Some days ago, I was helping my son with his homework as he researched the famous North American inventor, Thomas Edison. There are many inspiring aspects to his life story. For example, the number of inventions registered in his name is astounding. There are so many essential items whose existence we owe to him, like the light bulb, or cinema cameras, that the massive impact that Thomas Edison caused is still affecting all of our lives.

He also famously declared: "I have not failed. I've just found ten thousand ways that won't work". His stubborn determination and refusal to give up on the light bulb made him famous. His attitude was the key to the completion of that project which still benefits us all to this day. I believe this quote says a lot about how we should operate in the face of apparent defeat. Thomas Edison, it seems, faced it with a "challenge accepted" attitude and moved on.

Each one of us, however, has a different reaction to failure. Of course, in Edison's case, we are talking about a defeat restricted to a project or experiment, which is fairly technical and abstract. Some experiences of personal failure can be highly debilitating, to the point where we might even think we won't ever recover from them.

I believe all of us have some experience of defeat, one way or the other. I have been through seasons in my life that were so dark that I didn't think it would be possible for me to recover. When we hit rock bottom, and the world seems to fall apart, and we're frustrated and disappointed with everything or even with ourselves, we may think we will never get out.

Many are, in reality, unable to get out. Indeed, I believe it's impossible to survive a situation like this alone. I thank God for the people around us, who pray for us, support and help us. When we're at the end of ourselves and we see a Light, and we find out that God hasn't given up on us yet even if we have given up ourselves, the grace of God becomes a mark that is so deep in our souls that it can sustain us, raise us and bring us back to life.

That's an experience that only the true Gospel can produce in us. The true Gospel is the good news of salvation, in which all humanity is equally condemned, where all work by human hands is flawed, and we all need a saviour. The true Gospel has Jesus at the centre of it all, and He is the one who paid our debt in full. Through this true Gospel, we received the Holy Spirit who lives in us, which is the very power of God who resurrected Christ. In this true Gospel, there's no judgement, human betterment or promotion, and in it, I'll always be weak while He will always be strong. In this true Gospel we're free to receive the victory from the one who has overcome, Jesus Christ.

In this Gospel, I can declare: "I have been crucified with Christ and I no longer live, but Christ lives in me. The life I now live in the body, I live by faith in the Son of God, who loved me and gave himself for me."[43]This is the Gospel, the victory of the Cross in me. This is the Gospel that gives Him the Glory and has its foundation on His mercy and grace. Through this Gospel, I now have a relationship with life, not death. And then I can, symbolically, eat from the tree of life and not from the tree of right and wrong any more.

We all need this experience, this relationship with victory. We will, of course, face situations where we will

---

43 Galatians 2:20.

feel like a failure but, when we experience the victory in Him, we will find the strength to move forward.

To comprehend what this experience represents in greater depth, let's look at Peter's story, from the days that followed the crucifixion of Jesus.

It was the third day after Jesus' death, and some women bought spices and decided to visit his tomb to anoint his body. While walking, they asked each other who would help them roll the stone away from the tomb entrance.

When they got there, however, they found the stone removed. Jesus was not there, but an angel warned them he had risen. Jesus had risen!

The Gospel of Matthew tells us, "Then go quickly and tell his disciples, 'He has risen from the dead and is going ahead of you into Galilee. There you will see him.' Now I have told you."[44]

However, the narrative of Mark narrates the same episode, but with a subtle difference. The passage reads: "but go, tell his disciples and Peter"[45]. Why would Mark make this specific distinction of Peter's name, while Matthew didn't bother to mention this detail? Why would he even mention Peter's name if the angel was already calling all disciples? How is this distinction relevant?

---

44 Matthew 28:7.

45 Mark 16:7.

Why would the angel bother to make a mention of Peter at all?

Accordingly to theologians and Bible scholars, the apostle Peter would have been the source for all the information in Mark's Gospel. This Gospel would be a recording made by Mark from what he would have heard from Peter's mouth.

A small remark like this could be missing from other witnesses' accounts, which is acceptable. For Peter, though, more than to anybody else, that specific mention of his name was not only unforgettable but essential.

We need to understand Peter was not living his best days when he got notified about Jesus's resurrection. He was actually living out his worst days. The mention of his name was not an honourable mention, it was more of a surprise. For Peter, it was like a lifeline. The last thing he would have expected was to be mentioned or named for anything.

When everything seems lost

Only three days earlier, Peter had denied Jesus. As if that wasn't enough, he had done it three times, and worse, during the events that culminated in the condemnation and subsequent death of Jesus. Peter ruined everything and in the worst of all possible moments. He had failed Christ and himself.

Have you ever felt as if your mistake was so severe that there was no way out? Have you ever been on the verge of quitting? Have you ever felt completely defeated? They were all devastated by Jesus' death, but Peter was dying inside because of his failure.

Have you, at any point in your life, faced a situation like this? Have you ever made a total commitment to something, only to abandon it without ceremony? Have you ever let your soul take control even before you realised what you were doing?

Peter looked in the mirror and remembered the man who just a few instants before had said, "If I have to die with You, I will not deny You!"[46]. So, when he came to himself, he had already disowned Him three times. How did Peter see himself then? Probably a long way from that brave man who thought he was so full of faith.

Let's see the complete narrative of this event: "Peter said to Him, 'Even if all are made to stumble, yet I will not be.' Jesus said to him, 'Assuredly, I say to you that today, even this night, before the rooster crows twice, you will deny Me three times.' but he spoke more vehemently,

---

46 Mark 14:31 NKJV.

'If I have to die with You, I will not deny You!' and they all said likewise."[47]

And just like Peter failed, you and I can also fail today. Have you ever failed on a commitment or vow you made to God or yourself? If so, how did it make you feel? We may experience failure in many areas of our lives, but whatever the context, the pain it causes is debilitating, and the feeling of defeat may become paralysing. How can we recover from a situation like this? Peter failed God's very own Son, so how could it have even been possible for God to forgive him?

I remember always being a good student during my school years. I always did well and got good grades. I was never good, though, in the physical education classes. Those were my "cross" to bear. For the best part of my school years I was able to claim that I never had poor grades and that I never had to take a remedial class[48].

Until one day, it happened. In physical education, the course all my colleagues would sail through, smiling and relaxed, I was struggling. I remember we had to a pass an exam, and it wasn't much; I only had to run a few rounds on the athletics track. My problem was that I

---

47 Mark 14:29-31 NKJV.

48 NT: The original in Portuguese reads "ficado em recuperação", indicating a practice in Brazilian education that the student has to take remedial classes and additional exams to recover from not achieving the required grade.

avoided the PE classes more than anything. Still, I didn't want that stain on my CV, and failure in that class was not a pleasant feeling. Even in the little things failure makes us feel bad.

How many of us have experienced defeat while going through a diet, exercising and moving towards a healthier lifestyle? We set goals, count calories, prepare menus, set limits and make a strict shopping list. Then, suddenly, when we least expect, we've broken the diet and lost control. And before we notice, our will and desires have retaken control.

Another example can be our prayer and devotional routines. I once heard a pastor telling his testimony of how difficult it was for him to wake up early to have his devotional time. He said he recorded a cassette tape and used that as his alarm every day. In that recording, he would remind himself about the importance of separating that time to be with God. This is an area in which many of us Christians have failed. We might set a specific time to pray, read the Bible, and have a relationship with the Holy Spirit but, when the time comes, something else always tries to steal that time from us.

How do we cope with failure in our lives? What about when we fail in our profession, businesses or studies? What about when we fail with our family, children, or spouse? What about the feeling of defeat that comes when we fail with God? How can we recover from failures in these areas that are so essential in our lives?

The key in all these things is that we will always feel oppressed and depressed by our faults or failures, whatever the cause for them is. The Bible tells us about how Peter reacted in the face of his defeat, "Peter replied, 'Man, I don't know what you're talking about!' Just as he was speaking, the cock crowed. The Lord turned and looked straight at Peter. Then Peter remembered the word the Lord had spoken to him, "Before the cock crows today, you will disown me three times.' And he went outside and wept bitterly."[49]

We can give many more examples, but we always see defeat, which afflicts us so much, is constantly caused by our own souls.

In other words, our desires and instincts take control without any warning and cause us to turn back on our resolutions and take us down from our strong position. We are betrayed by ourself, by our own souls. Very appropriately, the prophet Jeremiah warns us about how deceitful our heart is[50].

---

49 Luke 22:60-62.

50 "The heart is deceitful above all things, and desperately wicked; who can know it?", Jeremiah 17:9 NKJV.

Peter wanted to be a good Christian. He even had a good CV already. Moreover, Peter had heard the Master declare spectacular promises to him. Jesus had previously said, "And I tell you that you are Peter, and on this rock I will build my church, and the gates of Hades will not overcome it."[51]

Note that Peter was not even his real name. It was Jesus who first called him that. His name was Simon, but when Jesus saw him for the first time, he said, "You are Simon son of John. You will be called Cephas (which, when translated, is Peter)"[52]. For Simon, to be called Peter, which means "rock", was a sign of honour, of distinction. He probably thought that even Jesus saw him like the strong man he was. The Master himself saw his value, strength and character.

It might be more challenging for us in the West to comprehend the context and depth of what Jesus' words meant for Peter's life. I started to understand a bit more after reading the commentary presented by a North American rabbi called Steve Bob. He mentions a Jewish tradition that says, "there are three names by which a person is called: one that his father and mother call him, one that other people call him, and one that he earns for himself. The best of all is the one that he earns for

51 Matthew 16:18.

52 John 1:42.

himself"[53]. To me, this is the context we need to understand the Jewish way of thinking and what was happening in Peter's mind.

Thus, the name my parents gave me is Saulo, which by chance also has its origins in the Hebrew language. It means "one who has been obtained through many prayers and supplication". I don't believe my parents were aware of this meaning when they chose this name, but I think that, in a way, their choice was absolutely right. When I was still a toddler, I suffered from a very high fever and seizures that almost killed me. My parents told me about their desperation and how that event caused them to seek God and cry out to Him for a miracle, as they were utterly hopeless.

There are still other names by which I'm known to people. I am called "son", "husband", and "dad". There are also other names we obtain from the context we're living. Some may call me "brother", "pastor", or "evangelist". Apart from that, no matter which name people come to know me by, I believe my real identity is the one God declares over me.

A famous worship song from *Hillsong Church* declares, "I am chosen, not forsaken, I am who You say I

53 *Tanhuma, Parshat Vayak'hel.*

am"[54]. I believe this profoundly defines our identity. We are what He declares us to be, and this is the name by which we should live. Interestingly, the grace of God goes against the Jewish tradition and does not expect us to earn this new name, but God had taken the first step even when we were lost in our sins.

Simon, then Peter, laboured to live up to those words of Jesus. With all his heart, he devoted himself to this task. Peter decided to devote himself to God with all his strength. He strived to keep the status of what that name meant. In the same way, good Christians, men and women who pursue God's will, tend to put themselves under a certain pressure.

Peter dealt with the situation in the only way he knew. He put even more pressure upon himself, setting the bar slightly higher. He would labour even harder to reach it, to be the first, the most pious, the most devoted, the bravest, the most trustworthy, the most unshakable, like a stone, like a solid rock.

And Peter never thought he would fail. He never imagined he would be able to do what he did, simply disowning Jesus in such a cheap way. Up to that moment, Peter thought he could live up to the Master's words. He believed that if Jesus had said it, it was because of

---

54 *"I am chosen, not forsaken, I am who You say I am"*
Who You Say I Am © Hillsong Publishing, by Reuben Timothy Morgan and Benjamin David Fielding.

Peter's personal merits. So when Peter failed, his world fell apart, his trust in himself crumbled, and he thought it was the end. In his heart, he was disqualified for every purpose God could have.

In his mind, Peter had ruined everything: wasted all his chances, all his hopes, his CV, his honour and all his strength. He didn't feel any better than the traitor Judas. How could he even imagine going again? How could God possibly want him back or include him in His plans?

Another character from the Bible went through a similar experience. Jonah, the prophet, could well have earned himself the name "fleeing prophet", when he abandoned the Lord's command. I was surprised, however, when I first read what he said: "What I have vowed I will make good."[55]. This statement indicates that Jonah indeed said "yes" once to God. He didn't refuse to do God's will at first. Then, however, something happened midway. His own will took control and carried him in the opposite direction to the purposes of God.

The Bible doesn't tell us much about who Jonah was, but it gives us some hints. He is mentioned as a prophet during the kingdom of Jeroboam[56], and it's also very likely that Jonah had been one of the "sons of prophets"

---

55 Jonah 2:9.

56 2 Kings 14:25.

trained by Elisha[57] himself. Accordingly to a Jewish tradition, Jonah was the son of the woman from Shunem. The son who died and was brought back to life by Elisha. He is called the "son of Amitai", which also means "son of the Truth".

Like Peter, Jonah also had a reputation to keep and a solid and meaningful name to earn. So, what caused Jonah to fall from this place and position himself as the adversary to his own calling? I find it very interesting how God decided to give Jonah more than one chance. God could have just left Jonah to one side and called another prophet.

The first chance Jonah got was the storm. Some apocryphal Jewish writings even suggest the storm was centred directly and exclusively over the boat he was in and that all other ships would have been able to move around peacefully. You and I may also go through storms. Sometimes, it looks like we're the only ones going through problems, while everything is going well for everybody else.

Jonah didn't take his chance. The storm could have put him on the right path, but he hadn't yet repented. Instead, Jonah stubbornly persevered against God and even asked the sailors to throw him out into the sea. It was as if by his actions he was saying, "You can kill me if

---

57 2 Kings 6:1-7.

you want, but I'll still refuse to do what you asked me to do".

I think, however, that Jonah couldn't see any possibility of return. Maybe he thought that what he had done was so terrible that there would be no mercy available for him. Jonah might have looked at himself and said, "It doesn't matter anyway, I've messed it all up; God would never forgive me; I will never be able to get a second chance".

There's a saying that "nobody is completely useless if he sets a bad example". Considering the number of his errors, Jonah seems to have gained his place in the Bible only to show us what we shouldn't do. Jonah really ruined everything. He took a route of no return, a path without any hope. In his mind, Jonah might have already decided that God would not take him back. To him, the storm represented the beginning of all the punishment he surely deserved rather than a chance to return to God's plan. The only thing left for him was to wish death to come faster and the suffering to end.

Around him, while the boat was almost sinking and the ocean raging, lots were cast. A Jewish commentator from the Middle Ages, Isaac Abarbanel[58], says the idea that the sailors would trust in a simple act of casting lots

---

58 Isaac Abarbanel (1437-1508), referenced by Steven Bob, in *"Jonah and the meaning of our lives"*, The Jewish Publication Society, Philadelphia, 2016.

seemed absurd. So he proposed that they must have cast lots many times and that in all of them, the lot fell on Jonah, like some sort of statistical aberration that could not be ignored.

Whatever the case, he was exposed mid-flight and had to reveal what was eating him up, condemning him and bringing him shame. Abarbanel also goes far beyond and proposes that when Jonah had said "I am Hebrew", this expression would have dual intent. The word "Hebrew" (in Hebrew, *"ivri"*) has its roots in *"eiyin"*, *"vet"* and *"raish"*, from which you can form another word, *"aveira"*, which means "sin". So when Jonah said *"ivri anochi"*, he would be declaring his identity as a Hebrew, and at the same time, he would be saying, "I am a sinner".

Jonah saw the reality of his soul and recognised his situation. He saw that all was lost, how he was to blame for it, and how his strength was now depleted. There was only one solution, one thing left to do. He surrendered to being thrown to his death. The sailors resisted as much as they could but finally, they also submitted to the force of the storm and threw Jonah into the sea to die.

To everyone who witnessed that moment, Jonah had died. Can you imagine these men coming back to their land and the stories they told? In the first place, the news of the man Jonah, the prophet, who had died.

Next, Jonah's relatives would likely be notified and would mourn him. Then, finally, the word would spread about the circumstances in which Jonah had died, of how he had disobeyed and fled from God. Jonah's entire reputation that he had built, as a man of God, would have been crushed in a moment. Jonah's faults had been exposed to whoever wanted to see them. Jonah's life was indeed over, his legacy destroyed.

Just like Peter, Jonah became a model of those who seemed to deserve nothing more than condemnation. He had finally been swallowed by a huge fish and, wrapped in the animal's gut, stayed in the ocean's darkness for three days. Some say that Jonah actually died, and his journey was an analogy for his descent to the depths of death. No matter how we interpret it, the undeniable fact is that Jonah was over.

The light shines in the darkness

My father, Tirso de Mello Santos, has served the Church for many years as a pastor, a prophet and a worship leader. One of the characteristics of his ministry as a worship leader is that he writes songs that are also the story of his own life, recording his scars and his experiences with the Holy Spirit.

A few years ago, my parents were working for God, planting a church in Porto Alegre, in Rio Grande do Sul[59]. God had clearly guided them into that city, and they were ready to obey. Despite the fact that they weren't young, they had left the comfort of a stable life and ministry in Curitiba[60] to venture into new territory. They gave up everything to obey God's voice.

However, the level of opposition they faced was not something they were expecting. The church plant seemed to be going in the right direction until one day when great dissension started amongst it's founding members. My parents suffered a fierce challenge to their authority as pastors and leaders. It was a fight they didn't enlist for and a very sad, dark and lonely moment.

In the middle of the pain and doubt, my dad wrote a song that says, "When everything seems lost, all questions are unanswered; I look for a hidden fruit, but the tree now has none; when I cry but I can't hear any answer, I can only hear my own voice clearly, there's nothing I can do, other than waiting on You; I let myself go by Your hand, all I want is to surrender everything at Your feet,

---

59 TN: Porto Alegre is the capital city of the state of Rio Grande do Sul, which is the most southern state in Brazil.

60 TN: The capital city of the state of Parana, in Brazil.

and I try to quiet down my heart, with a certainty that everything will change in You"[61].

That song, born from that moment of pain, has blessed so many people, helping them find hope and perspective. Sometimes we can't comprehend the reason behind the problems and challenges we go through, but we know that there's a place of hope if our lives are in God's hands.

Peter was stuck in anguish, thinking that there was no hope for him. Peter had stayed in this darkness for three days. Jonah remained in the belly of the death, in the deep darkness of the seas for three days. Both thought that everything was lost. Both saw only darkness. Both were suffering from depleted strength and resources.

Maybe you have also been through times like this when it seems impossible to see your hand in front of you, and it seems you're in dense darkness, as if there's no more hope or perspective. However, there is an amazing spiritual principle about darkness: "The light shines in the darkness, and the darkness has not overcome it"[62].

---

61 Quando Tudo Parece Perdido © Tirso de Mello Santos, from the album "Com o Rosto Descoberto".

62 John 1:5.

Jesus was dead for three days, but "In Him was life, and that life was the light of all mankind"[63]. Death could not hold him down because the "Light" shines in the darkness, and the darkness could not, in any way, defeat him. Death could not hold him down because Jesus was the very life, the very light.

Peter was right in the middle of his storm, anguish and suffering. He was in a place in his soul where he thought all was lost. Right there, though, Peter saw a great light. What he least expected or even imagined possible actually happened. A heavenly revelation came, a message from God himself that intentionally included him again in the Divine purpose. How could it be? The angel said his name, the same name Christ had given him, placing him back in the position he no longer deserved.

Peter came to know something new, a higher revelation. He was one of the first to experience the new work that Christ accomplished through his death and resurrection. Peter experienced first-hand the mercy and grace of God. Mercy, because Peter actually deserved condemnation, but he didn't get it. And grace, because what he did not deserve, he obtained.

And from within the thick darkness that Peter thought he would never get out of again, God decided to

---

63 John 1:4.

lead him out and into His plans again. Peter had lost hope and already given up on himself, but God, with that gesture, was making him aware that He hadn't given up on Peter. In the same way, He hasn't given up on you or me.

Maybe you and I have made the same mistakes several times. We want to be good Christians, but we constantly fail. We may even have accepted the state of defeat. Who knows, we might as well have already settled for condemnation and punishment as if conceding that God could never include us in his plans again. And then, we simply close our hearts to what God can do. As if the power that resurrected Christ from the dead could ever be limited! We might think there's salvation for us, but that's it. Surely the blessings He has for his children would not be available for us, not after the things we've done! But, in the middle of this valley of shadow and death, a powerful light shines.

Let's look, once again, to Jonah, "From inside the fish Jonah prayed to the Lord his God. He said: 'In my distress I called to the Lord, and he answered me. From deep in the realm of the dead I called for help, and you listened to my cry. You hurled me into the depths, into the very heart of the seas, and the currents swirled about me; all your waves and breakers swept over me. I said, 'I have been banished from your sight; yet I will look again towards your holy temple.' The engulfing waters threatened me, the deep surrounded me; seaweed was wrapped around my head. To the roots of the mountains I sank down; the earth beneath barred me in for ever. But you, Lord my God, brought my life up from the pit. 'When my life was ebbing away, I remembered you, Lord, and my prayer rose to you, to your holy temple. 'Those who cling to worthless idols turn away from God's love for them. But I, with shouts of grateful praise, will sacrifice to you. What I have vowed I will make good. I will say, 'Salvation comes from the Lord.'" And the Lord commanded the fish, and it vomited Jonah onto dry land."[64].

I confess that even having read the book of Jonah many times, it was only more recently that I noticed a subtlety in the structure of this second chapter that changed the whole meaning for me.

It's fascinating to see that when Jonah declared things like "I will look again towards your holy temple", and "brought my life up from the pit", and yet, "Salvation comes from the Lord", God hadn't yet given the orders for the fish to vomit him onto dry land.

Something had happened in Jonah's heart and spirit, that even before being vomited out by the fish, he was able to say these things. I always thought Jonah's prayer spanned two time periods. First, repentance and second,

---

64 Jonah 2:1-10.

gratitude, but only after being delivered from oppression. However, if we look more closely at the scripture, we see Jonah's thankfulness was not because he had been vomited out by the fish, that hadn't even happened yet.

Jonah was talking about something completely different. Jonah had messed everything up. Jonah had ruined every possibility for the plan of God to be accomplished in his life. As far as everyone else was concerned, Jonah was dead. But, more importantly, as far as Jonah was concerned, he was already dead. His recent actions had destroyed any hope of recovery.

Those who saw Jonah for the last time (as they supposed) witnessed his death, and maybe they had even seen the gigantic sea creature that came and swallowed Jonah. To an outside observer, it seemed as if it wasn't enough for God to punish him with a terrible death by drowning, but He also wanted him to be eaten alive. Only, what seemed like a double death sentence was, actually, one more chance God was giving to Jonah.

Right in the middle of this hopeless situation, and knowing that he had miserably failed God's plan for his life, a light shone right through Jonah's darkness. He realised God hadn't given up on him. Even though the whole world could have said that Jonah was dead and over, the wrong person for the job, with his reputation in ruins, God decided it wasn't the end yet.

In his prayer, Jonah speaks about his impossible situation, of how God had forgiven him and included him again in His plans. Jonah's thankfulness was about the deliverance of his soul, about having received forgiveness. He didn't expect his prayer to be heard by God, but when he did pray, the Lord immediately replied.

A few days ago, my wife and I went out for a walk. It was a beautiful spring day in Wales, and while we walked by a little old chapel near Roath in Cardiff, something caught our eye. There was a very old tree that had once been broken and brought down. I imagine it might have fallen during a storm, as they are fairly frequent around here.

This tree, however, was alive and vibrant. Its branches had continued to grow upward towards the light and the heat. Lots of tiny, beautiful purple flowers blossomed around that tree and over its exposed roots, which were still marked by scars from the storm that should have destroyed it.

The Holy Spirit reminded me of a scripture in the book of Job that says, "For there is hope for a tree, if it is cut down, that it will sprout again, and that its tender shoots will not cease"[65]. If there's hope for a tree, there's also hope for you and me. Our God hasn't forgotten us and hasn't given up on us.

---

65 Job 14:7 NKJV.

I've been through a similar experience myself and I too was in that valley of darkness and death once. It was a place I thought I'd never come out of. I also believed God could never have a place for me again in his plans and I thank God for the people who prayed for me and helped me get back on my feet. The events I've been through, my flaws, my scars are a constant reminder to me of my weakness. But, they are also a reminder of how strong God is in me and of His grace.

This constant reminder is so precious to me. For the same reason, God once said to Paul, "My grace is sufficient for you, for my power is made perfect in weakness"[66]. He doesn't take our weakness and our scars away. But, when he makes us see who we really are, we can stop living the illusion that we're perfect. We can then depend on him even more, every day. I can say, today, that I prefer to be the broken version of myself and no longer depend on myself, but only on Him who is stronger than me.

My heart aches for every one of my brothers and sisters, who have been called by God, and have served in His house, but then drifted away and fell. Who will help them to get up? If we, who are close, don't reach out, who will? Our function as the Lord's Church is to love

---

66 2 Corinthians 12:9.

and help those who once gave their lives for the love of the Gospel, and not to throw them to the wolves.

Just like God commanded the angel to say, "and Peter", he looks at you today and calls you by your name. While you still have air in your lungs, there's still hope. Peter, Jonah, and so many others were once in a place like this, but they saw a great light. God didn't give up on them and He hasn't given up on you.

The condition for surrendering

While reading Jonah's prayer before, some things seemed to be out of context. For example, I couldn't understand why Jonah suddenly mentioned idolatry when he says, "Those who cling to worthless idols turn away from God's love for them"[67]. This statement, however, is made at the peak of his joy and gratitude. Jonah had found mercy, grace, life and forgiveness and at that wonderful revelation, it was almost as if he was saying, "How could anybody despise that?" or yet, "How could I be so foolish, seeking these things and despising your mercy?". He found out that "mercy triumphs over judgement!"[68].

---

67 Jonah 2:8.

68 James 2:13.

The scripture continues, "But I, with shouts of grateful praise, will sacrifice to you. What I have vowed I will make good. I will say, 'Salvation comes from the Lord.'"[69]. In the middle of Jonah's chaos, God has revealed himself merciful. Right there, in the middle of Jonah's agony, God shone a powerful light. God's mercy in Jonah's life produced thankfulness.

I'm fascinated by the order in which these things happened. First, Jonah had an encounter with the grace of God, which produced thankfulness in him, and only then was he able to say, "What I have vowed I will make good". He was only able to find a place of surrender after that experience.

The revelation of God's grace and mercy produced thankfulness, which then produced surrender in Jonah's heart. What was once impossible for him because his own will was against it, he was finally able to do, after having recognised God's mercy and experiencing thankfulness. The most ruthless fight in a man's heart is to overcome one's own will. Jonah was able to overcome with the help of God's grace, mercy and thankfulness.

Allow me to try to clarify this even more. First, Jonah needed to face how much he was not. It was impossible for Jonah to even surrender to God's will while he thought highly about himself. The reality check of his

---

69 Jonah 2:9-10.

weakness was fundamental for him to start living the most extraordinary days of his life. Yet, now, broken down and with his reputation ruined, weak and defeated according to human standards and like a dead man, he rose again in the power of the one who can bring the dead back to life. He had done an impossible work, so off the charts that some biblical historians say it can't be literally true.

God is not waiting for perfect people with excellent CVs. God prefers to restore the broken, resurrect the dead and raise an army from a valley full of dried and scattered bones. What is impossible for this God? Who is too lost for Him? He hadn't given up on Jonah and neither does He give up on us.

Let's look again at Peter, who also had a defining moment: "When they had finished eating, Jesus said to Simon Peter, 'Simon son of John, do you love me more than these?' 'Yes, Lord,' he said, 'you know that I love you.' Jesus said, 'Feed my lambs.' Again Jesus said, 'Simon son of John, do you love me?' He answered, 'Yes, Lord, you know that I love you.' Jesus said, 'Take care of my sheep.' The third time he said to him, 'Simon son of John, do you love me?' Peter was hurt because Jesus asked him the third time, 'Do you love me?' He said,

'Lord, you know all things; you know that I love you.' Jesus said, 'Feed my sheep.'[70].

Some subtleties of the original manuscripts can't be seen in the English translation. For example, while there are two different words in the original text, the translation uses the expression "love". Peter, however, didn't even dare to use the same word Jesus used to describe love. Jesus asked his questions using the word "agape" (ἀγαπάω), which represents a love that is eternal, perfect, divine, unconditional, unlimited. And Peter, who once thought of himself as the strong one, answered using the word "*fileo*" (φιλῶ), which means a fraternal love, human, natural and essentially limited.

His life had been marked forever. He didn't even dare to define himself as a rock, unshakable. He didn't dare to raise himself above others. He knew his reality now; he knew how weak he was. He didn't try anymore to be greater than he was. He was the one who had once ruined everything and thrown all the good he had away, he was the one who didn't deserve anything. When he encountered God's grace and mercy and experienced thankfulness in his heart, he was able to surrender his own will and really live to fulfil his calling to take care of the Lord's sheep. He could now live up to the name Jesus once gave him. Simon thought the name "Peter"

70 John 21:15-17.

was because he was strong, but he found out that strength could only come from surrendering to the one who was stronger than him, the true, unshakable Rock.

He doesn't give up on us

I don't know the circumstances you are living in now. I don't know if you've been through a valley like this, or maybe you're still in it, a valley of shadow and darkness, like the one Jonah and Peter were in. One thing, though, I know: our Lord went through that same valley of shadow and death, but death could not hold him!

The whole of humanity was a lost cause, yet God didn't give up on us. Jesus said, "The kingdom of heaven is like treasure hidden in a field. When a man found it, he hid it again, and then in his joy went and sold all he had and bought that field."[71].

When no one else saw value, our God did. When no one else saw hope, our God did. When no one else saw love, our God loved. Where there was only darkness, our God shone a powerful light.

Even if we have thought about giving up many times over, we need to understand that He doesn't give up on us! What he did for you and me was not a small thing.

---

71 Matthew 13:44.

He died because of us and was resurrected because of us! He gave up everything, paid our debt and settled it completely! He gave us a calling, mission and purpose! He gave us his own life!

Today, we can rise from the valley of shadow and death! God's mercy and grace are the only pre-requisites for doing God's work.

"Arise, shine; for your light has come! And the glory of the Lord is risen upon you. For behold, the darkness shall cover the earth, and deep darkness the people; but the Lord will arise over you, and His glory will be seen upon you."[72]

---

72 Isaiah 60:1-2 NKJV.

ADJUSTING THE FOCUS

I heard somebody saying Jonah was the most successful preacher and evangelist of all history. He was the only one to get 100% positive responses for his preaching. Not just a few people, but an entire town converted from their evil ways on a single day. Not even Billy Graham got such an impressive result, even on his best days.

Even though Jonah seemed like the wrong choice, unfit for the task, and even after having done it all wrong, how was it possible that Jonah fulfilled God's calling? God never gave up on him, but can we grasp the fact that Jonah's achievements were so outstanding that nobody after him was ever able to match them? We've already seen how he proved himself unworthy and all the reasons why he didn't deserve it. So why would God give him so much of His power and allow such great results?

Our natural inclination is to look for clues in Jonah's history and behaviour to explain how he became acceptable to God. Common sense says that people get what they deserve. Some call it *"karma"*.

In the Church, as the body of Christ, we make the mistake of applying the same mentality, even though it's the direct opposite of God's mindset. We judge each other and say that if somebody is going through a rough patch, it's because he must have done something wrong. We judge the sinner as if we didn't sin ourselves. For example, if God uses us with gifts of healing, miracles, prophecies, etc., we secretly reflect on how much we deserve God's anointing, because we're "such a good person". People will look and talk about how a person is a holy man or woman of God, so good and so perfect. We've had too many scandals in the history of the Church to know that it simply is not like that.

Jonah had done everything wrong and wasn't included in God's plans on his own merits. In fact, he didn't seem to have any. Maybe that was why! Jonah, as a person, didn't have an identity or a reputation. He was incapable of carrying out his mission. However, God got him there anyway. Jonah didn't even have physical strength, or mental and emotional energy for what was up ahead. Yet, when he positioned himself to go in the direction of God's calling, simply obeying his voice, the supernatural power of God moved.

Just imagine the scene: Jonah shows up in the middle of a foreign city, with his hair wild, barefoot, clothes reeking of the foul smell of rotten fish. Possibly, people had heard stories from the sailors about a foreign prophet that had died, but here he was, back from the dead, prophesying against the city.

Jonah had no merit or strength left. He couldn't possibly depend upon himself anymore. A man with strong opinions, persistent, stubborn even, came to the end of his strength and finally surrendered. He couldn't depend upon himself anymore as it was practically impossible at that stage. It was from this very place that the power of God worked through Jonah so greatly that it earned its place as one of the most impressive stories in the Bible.

If you and I think that calling and ministry have anything to do with our own merits and experience, we're going down a path that is far from reality. If we believe we are good, and that's why God called us, we couldn't be more mistaken.

Throughout the Bible and the history of the Church, God has repeatedly chosen people that the world rejected. God chooses the ones He wants, not according to merit, but by His grace and power. He expects us to understand that. If we depend upon Him with all our hearts, we will start to see the "greater works" in our days. Everything starts when we find the end of ourselves. Our starting point, our foundation, is knowing how much we are not and how much He is.

Ron Kenoly recorded, in 1994, a song that says, "if You can use anything, Lord, You can use me"[73]. I remember the first time I heard this song. The notion that God can use whatever He chooses and the realisation that I fit in the category of "anything" filled me with fear and wonder. I was stunned but also amazed by God's power and greatness.

There is nothing that a human being can do for God if it's not through God himself, by his Holy Spirit. So, all those called by God to do something are also equally incompetent to perform it.

Look at David, for example, the shepherd boy who, without any training, was commissioned by God to fight against a giant using only a piece of leather and a stone. Or how about Moses, the stuttering older man, a wanted assassin? Moses, who had wasted a good part of his life, was called to go against the most powerful kingdom on Earth at the time and to miraculously free God's people from the slavery which had oppressed them for more than 400 years.

---

73 *"If You can use anything Lord You can use me"*
Use me © Universal Music Publishing Group, by Bill Withers.

Or Gideon, the least in his father's house who was cowardly threshing wheat in a winepress. He was visited by an angel of the Lord and became a great warrior and deliverer. Then there were Abraham and Sarah, who, at more than a hundred years old, gave birth to a child because God had called them to be the parents of a great people.

Time after time, generation after generation, God calls those who are nothing, as if they were something[74]. He lifts them and gives them life and power, even though he knows we are only dust. Look at the example of Jonah, who, even after having been powerfully used by God, was still Jonah, the man. It's comforting to me that Jonah still got his priorities wrong, mourning the loss of the comfortable shade for his head, while a whole city was at risk of being destroyed[75].

God doesn't call us because we are good. We are regularly in a battle against ourselves. One moment, we're moved by eternity and the next instant, we're moved by ourselves. God is never shocked by our humanity but he chooses not to erase our weaknesses. As

---

74 "But God chose the foolish things of the world to shame the wise; God chose the weak things of the world to shame the strong. God chose the lowly things of this world and the despised things – and the things that are not – to nullify the things that are, so that no one may boast before him." 1 Corinthians 1:27-29.

75 Jonah 4:6-11.

Paul once asked, why doesn't he simply remove our "thorn in the flesh"[76]?

I believe God's answer to Paul also applies to all of us today: His grace is enough for us. We need to know that we're weak and He is strong. We need to know we depend on Him. We need to know that it's not about us so that we don't exalt ourselves and lose focus. We need the knowledge that man does not live on bread alone but on every word that comes from the mouth of God[77].

For such a time as this

One of the stories from the Bible that best illustrates this is that of Esther. This young Jewish girl became queen of the Persian empire and God brought great deliverance and salvation for His people through her.

---

76 "Therefore, in order to keep me from becoming conceited, I was given a thorn in my flesh, a messenger of Satan, to torment me. Three times I pleaded with the Lord to take it away from me. But he said to me, 'My grace is sufficient for you, for my power is made perfect in weakness.' Therefore I will boast all the more gladly about my weaknesses, so that Christ's power may rest on me." 2 Corinthians 12:7-9.

77 "Jesus answered, 'It is written: "Man shall not live on bread alone, but on every word that comes from the mouth of God."'." Matthew 4:4.

Her story is recorded in the book of the Bible that bears her name.

Esther was a young lady like any other. She was just an ordinary girl. Esther didn't have noble descent, wealth, or anything else that would make her stand out as the obvious candidate for the position she eventually achieved. On the contrary, since she was a Jew, she was considered a second-class citizen.

Throughout history, the Jewish people have probably been the most persecuted people on Earth. They were hated by many and enslaved by others. More than once, their complete extinction was planned. We don't need to go too far in the past to find many examples of this. The most obvious and dramatic was the genocide of six million Jews at the hands of the German Nazis during the Second World War, which represented approximately sixty per cent of all the Jewish population in Europe at the time[78].

In the context of the book of Esther, the Jewish people were being oppressed and enslaved once more. They had been taken into exile into Babylon, against their will, by Nebuchadnezzar. In the middle of a strange and idolatrous nation, away from their land, being Jewish

---

78 *"The 'Final Solution': Estimated Number of Jews Killed"*, The Jewish Virtual Library; https://www.jewishvirtuallibrary.org/ estimated-number-of-jews-killed-in-the-final-solution; accessed in 31/5/2021.

was not an advantage to them. Their sole purpose in that place was to serve; they were a social class without any perspective. Esther's cousin and adoptive father, Mordecai, even instructed her to hide her origins.

Nowadays, social mobility is more of a thing. There are numerous examples of people who started from nothing and became very successful, even leaders in society. There is also more flexibility in our days for social mobility in the more orthodox contexts. For example, in the United Kingdom, we saw in May 2018 the wedding of Prince Harry with the "commoner" Meghan Markle, a mixed race actress and Hollywood star. In times past, the association of royalty with anybody who didn't have a noble lineage would have been totally unacceptable. In the old days, kingdoms were built on arranged marriages with only political purposes.

If we go back in time to when Esther was living, approximately two thousand, five hundred years ago, social mobility was utterly impossible. One who was born a noble would remain a noble. Also, anyone who was born a commoner would remain a commoner. In the same way, anyone born a slave would always be a slave.

Esther had one more significant limitation: She was a woman. Nowadays, women can take any opportunity or any kind of job. But, in those days, women were only expected to perform certain roles. The role of the woman was to serve her husband and bear children. So there was Esther, in this context, with no expectation for the future. She certainly could never imagine what was ahead of her and what the future would hold.

However, in a surprising, sudden and unprecedented way, a royal decree changed everything. It always amuses me, even annoys me a little, when I see some of the biblical movies around. I've seen several movies and cartoons about Esther. Unfortunately, the vast majority dramatise her story inaccurately. I remember one of them, for example, that showed Esther being dragged by force out of the house by soldiers while Mordecai was shouting and trying desperately to save her. Maybe there was a reason for that drama in the movie, but since I'm not a cinema critic, let's not go there! One thing I know: this is not the same story described in the Bible.

For Esther and all other young ladies in the kingdom, that decree was the opportunity of a lifetime. It was an incredible event, something extraordinary. So many girls dream about becoming princesses, living in a castle and marrying a prince. How many opportunities like this really exist? It's not like you could find an advert on a job board: "Princess needed for marriage. If interested, please attend the royal ball".

Now, there it was, right before Esther, precisely that opportunity. It didn't only mean she would be able to leave a life of servanthood, but it would give her the highest social status available in the world at that time.

What could compare to living in the palace? Imagine having all the best stylists at your disposal, the best clothes, the very best cosmetics, the finest perfumes, the best shoes, all the comfort and luxury one could dream of and more. Any woman in her situation would have done the same as she did. She launched herself into that project, body and soul, and devoted her best to winning that great contest.

The Bible tells us about each step involved in the long preparation process, and how she worked to be the best. Thanks to the advantage of having God's favour, she found grace with people, and was finally accepted in the king's presence. The king was pleased with her and made her his queen. Amongst all the other women from the highest social classes, the former slave had become the most important, above all others. Esther was now Queen Esther.

While contemplating all the luxury and honour that the position would carry, Esther could have said: "God loves me!" God indeed loved her, and she knew it. God had favoured her. God, undoubtedly, had a plan. God loved her to the point of fulfilling all the dreams a little girl could dream: God had made her a princess and a queen! So, surrounded by all luxury and honour, she couldn't dream any bigger.

Now, how much did she really understand about the meaning of her purpose? She could think God was simply pleased with her because she was a good girl, who respected people and loved God, and for that reason, God had decided to reward her. God had put her in a position of great honour, but Esther did not realise the significance of what she had received.

In the middle of that beautiful princess dream, an unexpected event happened. The biblical narrative tells us that, "In every province to which the edict and order of the king came, there was great mourning among the Jews, with fasting, weeping and wailing. Many lay in sackcloth and ashes. When Esther's eunuchs and female attendants came and told her about Mordecai, she was in great distress. She sent clothes for him to put on instead of his sackcloth, but he would not accept them. Then Esther summoned Hathak, one of the king's eunuchs assigned to attend her, and ordered him to find out what was troubling Mordecai and why. So Hathak went out to Mordecai in the open square of the city in front of the king's gate."[79].

All that turmoil disturbed Esther in the middle of her dream. The most incredible part of it was that she didn't even know what was afflicting her cousin, Mordecai. All Jews in every province were desperate about this decree

---

79 Esther 4:3-6.

that was effectively a death sentence, but she, alienated from everything, wasn't even aware that there was a crisis. Mordecai, however, was desperate before God, fasting in sackcloth.

Esther couldn't understand why he was doing all that. She even sent him clothes. After all, her closest relative was making a scene at the palace doors. It was really humiliating. What would others think of her if they found out that the man dressed like a drifter, disturbing the palace routine, was, in reality, her relative, her cousin, or worse, someone she regarded as a father?

He was affecting her social status. After all, who did he think he was, coming to the palace's doors like that? To make matters worse, as well as causing a disturbance, he was there to ask her to do something impossible, which could lead to her death. There was a law at the time that unless the king extended the gold sceptre towards the person who came into his presence, any intruder would be immediately killed. And it had already been a month since the king had called her.

The biblical narrative continues: "Then she instructed him to say to Mordecai, 'All the king's officials and the people of the royal provinces know that for any man or woman who approaches the king in the inner court without being summoned the king has but one law. They will be put to death unless the king extends the gold sceptre to them and spares their lives. But thirty days have passed since I was called to go to the king.'"[80]

Esther's probably thought, "Ok, it's fine that there's a crisis and that people are going to die, but why is it all of a sudden my problem? What do I have to do with all this? What could I possibly do about it? Look, I have my commitments already, my calendar; after all, being the queen is hard work! There are banquets I need to organise. There are events to be planned. And, on top of that, I need to continuously work to keep myself the most beautiful in the kingdom. After all, I'm the queen!" She couldn't possibly agree with her stepfather.

She had her own opinion about the subject and she had more important things to do. Indeed, wouldn't it be easier for Mordecai to take care of this? Surely there must be someone else better prepared for this mission? She could have come up with a thousand excuses, some of which we might recognise: "My time is so limited! I have a job; I am the queen! Let some 'full-time Jew' take care of this! This can't be my responsibility! After all, if it becomes a burden it can't be right, can it?".

And the scripture continues: "When Esther's words were reported to Mordecai, he sent back this answer: 'Do not think that because you are in the king's house you alone of all the Jews will escape. For if you remain silent

---

80 Esther 4:10-11.

at this time, relief and deliverance for the Jews will arise from another place, but you and your father's family will perish. And who knows but that you have come to your royal position for such a time as this?'"[81]

When Mordecai said these words, "And who knows but that you have come to your royal position for such a time as this?", she was shocked. It was like her eyes finally opened. During the time she had been in the palace, she had thought everything was about her and the honour, the riches, the luxury and the comfort were gifts she had received for her enjoyment. She supposed her life and position, the favour and calling from God, were because of her and for her.

The confrontation made her experience the most significant shock of her life while realising that her position as a queen was not for her own luxury or glory. Her role as queen came with a service to perform. Her position included a commitment that was bigger than she had imagined. The responsibility it carried was so big that it would even require a willingness to die for her people.

Esther felt the weight of that moment and was shocked by the fact that now everything depended on her. Looking back over her people's history, she remembered the promises, the legacy, the patriarchs, Moses, the

---

81 Esther 4:12-14.

law, the kings and prophets. All of it was at stake if she didn't surrender to do what God called her to do. So, what was at risk now was vastly higher than herself and her comfort.

The labour and the promises of all the past generations were now in her hands. Without asking for it or realising, she now had received a baton, and there was a choice in her hands. She could fulfil God's purpose, for which she was called, even if that cost her her life, or she could lose her life trying to save it[82].

In the first days of 2013, my wife and I travelled to the United Kingdom for the first time. It had been several years since the Holy Spirit had spoken to us about His plans and purposes for our lives in this country. So it was with great joy and great expectation in God that I prepared to participate in an event called "School of Evangelism", organised by the ministry "Christ for All Nations"[83], founded by one of the heroes of faith from this generation, the Evangelist Reinhard Bonnke.

During that week, I was with a small group of people at the Kensington Temple church in Notting Hill, and it was one of the most important and meaningful moments

---

82 "For whoever wants to save their life will lose it, but whoever loses their life for me will find it." Matthew 16:25.

83 CfAN – *Christ for All Nations* (www.cfan.org).

of my life. Even before it started, I remember my wife shared with me that she felt from the Holy Spirit that a baton was being passed on. I had little understanding of how deep that was.

Each day, each session, we were ministered to by Reinhard Bonnke, Daniel Kolenda, Peter Vandenberg, Todd White and others, and there was a tangible and growing sense of the presence of the Holy Spirit in that place. I cannot explain it any other way, than that I had an impression in my spirit that something hugely important was about to happen, as if all my life events had built towards that very moment, towards something I couldn't yet comprehend.

When the Thursday evening session came, I understood. Brother Reinhard Bonnke started to tell us his experience of how he had come to London to study in the theological seminary. When he had been about to go back to Germany, and since he had a little time before catching his train, he had decided to enjoy the day in London. So he hopped on a bus at random, which got him to the neighbourhood of Clapham Common. He got out for a walk and found a house with a little plaque: "George Jeffreys residence".

He was astounded because he had learned a lot about that name. He knew and had read books about this fiery evangelist who God had powerfully touched in the Welsh revival, and later evangelised all over

England. This same George Jeffreys had also founded the denomination of churches called Elim, which exists to this day and is one of the largest Christian denominations in the United Kingdom.

He got filled with courage and decided to knock on the door. Reinhard asked and found out that it was indeed the house of that same George Jeffreys he had heard so many stories about. The person at the door didn't want to welcome him in at first, but from inside came a deep voice commanding to "let the young man come in".

Reinhard Bonnke was there, in the living room of that man who had done great things by the power of God in his generation. George Jeffreys barely talked but laid his hands over him and prayed, imparting the gift of the Holy Spirit. When he left that place, Reinhard got the bus back to the train station and then the train back home, to Germany. Shortly after, he heard the news that George Jeffreys had passed away.

There was great expectation in that room, as we all listened very attentively to this story. Reinhard then continued to say that only later did he realise the importance of that moment. When he received that prayer with the laying on of hands, he was actually receiving a baton. It was the same symbolism as in the book of Hebrews, chapter eleven, about a relay race, when a baton was placed in the hands of Peter and the apostles, then in Paul's hands. That same baton was in Luther's hands and in the hands of all the men and women who made themselves available for God to use them throughout history. This baton, which was also in the hands of men like Evan Roberts and George Jeffreys, was now being placed in his hands.

That event, that school of evangelism, didn't take the form of structured training. The sole purpose was to provide a heavenly moment for one generation to pass on the baton to the next generation. Reinhard told us how George Jeffreys was seventy-two years old when he died, and now Reinhard himself was the same age. He believed God had given him this special commissioning to pray, lay hands and pass the baton on.

A few years later, Reinhard Bonnke also passed away. Until now, almost nine years later, I remember that moment, and I'm filled with awe at the immense significance of that laying on of hands. The revelation that it is now my time, and this is my turn, still causes me to tremble. You and I are not isolated entities, we have a unique lineage. The Holy Spirit of God unites us. All of the Church's history brings us here to this very moment.

And just like Esther had realised it was her turn and her time had come, it's time for you and me to stand and do what God has been calling us to do. The time is now; the day is today. The baton is in our hands. It is time for us to get out of our hiding places, dare to hear the voice of the Holy Spirit, and move towards even greater things[84].

If Esther had rejected God's calling, Mordecai's words would have come to pass and God would have raised up another person to fulfil His plans, and the purpose for which God had created her would have been lost entirely; her life would have lost all sense and meaning. If you and I reject God's calling, that will never stop His purposes, but surely we will lose the very reason for our existence. God is eternal, so if our generation doesn't fulfil his plan, he can wait for another one. However, you and I only have now, and we can't give ourselves the luxury of waiting any longer.

Esther woke up. She heard the voice of God calling her name. She saw beyond herself and her own needs. Esther realised that everything that happened in her life till that day was indeed part of a plan. A plan that was not about herself, but the very plan of God, the same plan God is still building to today and has been since the beginning of time: His Church. The highest position Esther was destined to fill was not one of a queen but one of a servant.

---

84 "Very truly I tell you, whoever believes in me will do the works I have been doing, and they will do even greater things than these, because I am going to the Father." John 14:12.

When Esther woke up to the true purpose of her reign, she served God and her people at the risk of her own life. She could finally surrender and risk everything, but with an assurance that it would not be in vain. By doing this, Esther could honour those before her who had also given their lives and she saw God moving supernaturally in her generation. It's the same with you and me. When we wake up, we will also be able to see God's power in our days and honour all the generations of those who carried that precious baton before us.

Deep waters

The Word of God says: "The purpose in a man's heart is like deep water, but a man of understanding will draw it out."[85].

The Hebrew for "purpose", is *"etsah"*, which can have one of the following translations: purpose, plan, counsel, design, strategy, or plan by consequence of design.

This shows us that the very purpose of God, his very counsel, intent, design or divine strategy in which we're included, is present in our hearts from the very beginning. God compares these purposes with deep waters, i.e. something that needs to be explored and discovered.

---

85 Proverbs 20:5 ESVUK.

At first, the purpose of God for us is a mystery, but don't be fooled, His purposes are there. You and I are not an accident. God has a specific purpose established for our lives in this season. There is something in God that was prepared for us "for such a time as this". A baton is in my hands and your hands. This is our turn.

It was for such a time as this that God created us. For such a time as this, God has been positioning us where we are. Therefore, it is our honour and highest privilege to be living today and in this generation. Each day we get closer to the second coming of the Lord. Every day evil multiplies, but we also know from the scriptures that God will pour out even greater glory in these last days. Therefore, you and I can look forward to living in the most glorious days of the Church. This is our future. This is our destiny.

God's plans will never be frustrated. Whatever the Lord pleases, he does[86]. And that's how it is. The building of the Lord's house will be completed. The work God has started won't be interrupted.

And just like the baton was in Esther's hands, just like it was up to her whether or not to follow the purpose of her existence, it is in our hands today too.

Esther had the shock of her life when she found out that God had included her in His eternal purpose, and

---

86 "Whatever the Lord pleases, he does, in heaven and on earth, in the seas and all deeps.", Psalms 135:6 NKJV.

that He had commissioned her with such great responsibility, while she was the least likely candidate. She found out that it wasn't her abilities or skills that had brought her to that position of success, but rather that God himself had guided her at every step. Despite the shock, Esther chose to be available. She decided to trust. God has placed a calling and a purpose in my heart and yours. Maybe that comes as a shock to think that God would want to use us, even with our faults and weaknesses but it's time to explore those deep waters.

How can we know the purpose of God?

In Jonah's story, one of the episodes that I was always confused about was when God made a plant grow over Jonah's head and, later, let it it dry out. Jonah became utterly disheartened, even to the point of wanting to die. I really didn't understand the purpose of that story. Why would God make a plant grow and give Jonah shade only to make it die just after?

Also, God sent a hot wind. The original Hebrew word describes the wind as deafening, meaning a wind that is so powerful that it would silence any other sound. This wind, coming from the East, made the heat that day to be even more intense. In such extreme heat, Jonah would have had no energy for anything.

Who among us hasn't complained to God about a shade that was taken from over our heads? Or about a wind that blows unfavourably against us? How many of us have lost all our strength during some tribulation? We've all been through situations we don't understand and we question God about his motives. We have the option to let ourselves get upset, discouraged, angered or, like Jonah, even lose the will to live. We might even think, "If I'm doing God's work, how can it be that I'm going through a crisis like this?"

However, in such situations, God teaches us a precious lesson, just like he did with Jonah: His calling is not about us. The service God calls us to is not for our enjoyment and neither does it have the purpose of giving us shade. God's calling is to serve God and serve people. Using the example of the vine, God made Jonah see beyond his own interests and comfort and realise that there was a whole city, with a hundred and twenty thousand people on the verge of destruction.

By removing Jonah's shade, God opened Jonah's eyes and shared His own heart and feelings of compassion for those who were perishing. Like Jonah, we're also called to serve people, and God might as well take away the shade from above our heads if that's what's necessary for us to fulfil His plans.

By doing this, God is calling us to the highest position of all in His Kingdom, which is that of a servant: "But you are not to be like that. Instead, the greatest among you should be like the youngest, and the one who rules like the one who serves. For who is greater, the one who is at the table or the one who serves? Is it not the one who is at the table? But I am among you as one who serves."[87]

Thus, the first thing we need to find out about God's purposes for us is that it's not about us. We are not the centre, or the focal point. If God called you to be an entrepreneur, a pastor, a writer, an evangelist, a teacher, or whatever He has called you to do, it's really not about yourself. There is a purpose that is higher than you, and it's not about the shade above your head either. You will prosper, of course, because He is the one who called you. He not only gives us fair payment for our work, but He is also a rewarder. The plan of God, His overall purpose, is much greater than you and your happiness.

The plan of God for your life, primarily, is to Give Him glory. It's about honouring Jesus Christ. It's about making one name famous, that of Jesus. If you have looked at everything you've built and said, "God has blessed me", but you never asked yourself why, you might be taking a serious risk of passing through this life without fulfilling God's plans.

---

87 Luke 22:26-27.

One of the saddest things at the cemetery is not just the fact that a life has come to an end, and that they have run out of time. The most tragic thing for me is when we think about the potential buried there, the dreams and projects that never happened and the plans of God that never came to light in that life. Many people choose to save their own life and, when they least expect, they lose it[88]. Then the baton has to pass to the next generation because they were so busy and concerned about other things[89].

The purpose God wrote in our hearts is about blessing others and saving people. Esther was unaware of the reason behind Mordecai's affliction. She was unaware of the suffering of her own people and thought life was all about herself. Even the gesture of sending clothes to Mordecai was an act of self-love to stop her relative from embarrassing her, and to protect her honour.

However, God's plans for Esther were for His glory and for her to be a blessing to her brothers. She thought it was about her, but everything was about bringing honour to God and saving people.

---

88 "For whoever wants to save their life will lose it, but whoever loses their life for me will find it.", Matthew 16:25.

89 "'Martha, Martha,' the Lord answered, 'you are worried and upset about many things, but few things are needed – or indeed only one. Mary has chosen what is better, and it will not be taken away from her.'", Luke 10:41-42.

The purposes in a man's heart are compared to deep waters. Jesus said, "Whoever believes in me, as Scripture has said, rivers of living water will flow from within them"[90]. These waters are for quenching the thirst of many and not for us to keep stockpile for our own benefit.

Whether we ignore it, as Esther did, or not, the world around us is full of suffering. But there is a plan God has placed in my heart and yours to quench this thirst and bring glory to His name.

What is this plan, though? How can I know it? God doesn't want to hide His plans from us. It is in God's interest that you and I discover the purpose for which He has created us. He doesn't intend to keep it a mystery. Indeed, finding out about His plans has more to do with our attitudes and actions than God's.

God said "a man of understanding" draws them out. A man of understanding, insight, and wisdom can draw the purposes of God out from within the depths of his heart to bring them to life.

When you seek God for what He has determined for you, He will speak. Indeed, God is the one who puts dreams in our hearts. If you still don't have that vision, that revelation from God of what His purposes for you are, you need to seek Him and He will show you.

---

90 John 7:38.

God doesn't want you to live your whole life without living out His plans and dreams. He doesn't want you and I to be distracted like Esther once was, only never to wake up. His dreams are for such a time as this. They are for our present, for this generation.

But then, there is another step. When you get a glimpse of His plans and dreams for you, what can you do to draw them out? Scripture teaches us that wisdom and discernment are not only necessary for us to know what God has for us, but also for us to be able to draw it out. In other words, to convert a dream into something tangible and concrete.

We can often dream, imagine and get a glimpse of what He has prepared for us. However, not all of us can take these dreams further than their dream status by extracting these dreams out of our hearts for them to become a reality. Indeed, many take their dreams and projects to the grave without ever seeing them materialise.

The purposes in a man's heart are like deep waters. But drawing these waters out is not a simple task. If we go deeper into the parable, we will find out that digging a well involves a lot of hard work. First, one needs to remove the soil, debris and rocks. Then, when the correct depth is reached, pure water is found in the underground aquifers. However, this work never ends because every day it's necessary to draw more water out, which demands more effort.

This figure demonstrates that drawing out the dreams of God, which are written in our hearts, is no small task either and it will demand effort, dedication and surrender. Esther had realised that the cost was potentially her own life. Furthermore, she also realised that that was the very reason for her existence, and nothing else mattered. In the same way, we are faced with a choice, whether we wake up and draw out God's dreams or choose to waste our days living only for ourselves.

I know this seems harsh. However, the reality is that making a decision like this is not easy. We can spend days, months, years or even decades contemplating this choice and lack the strength and boldness to take a step forward. Is there a risk? Most certainly. Is there a price? Potentially, yes. How can we live in peace with ourselves if we don't try? How can we move ahead and pretend it has nothing to do with us?

I remember what I witnessed in my own home during my childhood and teenage years. My brothers and I witnessed how a calling from above transformed my parents' lives. We saw God moving in our home.

When I was little, my parents had good jobs in the banking sector, and we had a stable life, financially speaking. However, there was no peace, no purpose or sense in anything. My parent's marriage was on the verge of collapse, and our family was at risk. Yet, our family was restored when we found salvation in Christ and my brothers and I saw this happen.

After that, our lives took a very different turn. My parents invested all they had and entered a joint venture, a bakery. Their many dreams and business plans were upset by the hard reality of a partnership that didn't go well, and we ended up losing out. Then, on a much smaller scale, the company moved into our own house.

We had some challenging years. We didn't have access to many resources or privileges, and we all worked in our family business. Yet, in the middle of so much hard work (only those who have worked in this sector will know what I'm talking about) and while facing troubles and hardships, these were still the best days of our lives so far. So many songs that blessed so many lives were composed between one batch of bread and the next. So many friends received the gospel and were discipled right there. So many families were restored and transformed. There was now a purpose and a clear meaning to everything.

Increasingly, my parents gave themselves tirelessly to this mission. The calling from above was getting clearer and closer every day. Then, God touched their hearts, saying that "anybody could make bread, but not everybody could share the bread of life". And with all their hearts, they decided to launch themselves into this calling. Even when you've suffered through so many hardships, it's still not that simple to give up your only source of income.

In the same way that Peter was sure about water being liquid, we know that in this world we need resources to make our living. Listening to the voice of God, in a leap of faith, my parents obeyed and closed the bakery. A new season then started in our lives, which resulted in us knowing a deeper level of God's provision. Our life became a succession of miracles.

Although we didn't have "money", we'd been led to learn that we didn't need money. If we walk upon the "word that comes from God's mouth"[91], we'll walk upon much higher ground. We came to know a Bread, a level of provision that we had never encountered before (and neither our ancestors)[92]. I carry this with me until the present day. During hardships and struggles, we can now say our provision doesn't come from things but from every word that comes from God's mouth.

---

91 "Jesus answered, "It is written: 'Man shall not live on bread alone, but on every word that comes from the mouth of God.'", Matthew 4:4.

92 "He humbled you, causing you to hunger and then feeding you with manna, which neither you nor your ancestors had known, to teach you that man does not live on bread alone but on every word that comes from the mouth of the Lord.", Deuteronomy 8:3.

How can we reach this purpose?

So how can we reach the purposes God has for us? The first thing we need to do is to surrender. We must allow ourselves to be broken by the work of the cross. We will only be able to achieve the purposes of God for our lives if we're able to surrender our values and principles and give up our own lives. "Then Jesus said to his disciples, 'Whoever wants to be my disciple must deny themselves and take up their cross and follow me. For whoever wants to save their life will lose it, but whoever loses their life for me will find it. What good will it be for someone to gain the whole world, yet forfeit their soul? Or what can anyone give in exchange for their soul?"[93]

Note that when Jesus refers to losing your life, the word used in the Greek original is *"psychais"* (soul), which means he is talking about the soul and its manifestations: reason, will and emotions. Therefore, to reach the deep waters, we need to give up on what our heart desires and surrender to God's will. We cannot fulfil God's plans without giving up on our own plans. Similarly, we're also challenged to trust more in God's word than our own experience.

---

93 Matthew 16:24-26.

Peter, for instance, had all his experience against him when he decided to obey the words of Jesus. "'Come,' he said. Then Peter got down out of the boat, walked on the water and came towards Jesus."[94]. For a person who worked on the sea, the very idea of walking on the waters was absurd. Peter had entered those same waters thousands of times, and he had the absolute conviction that water was not solid. This step of faith required all the courage Peter had. However, when he decided to trust more in what Jesus said than in his own experience, he experienced something new, beyond his imagination.

The prophet Jonah, however, resisted God's voice. Whatever his reasons were, when he heard God's voice he decided to move in the opposite direction. In his wisdom and mercy, God continued to include Jonah in his plans, time after time. God challenges all legalist thought and shocks religious people. We, as humanity, are ready to judge and exclude people who have failed. However, God takes those who have failed and puts them back in the same place they were before they fell.

We can take comfort in the fact that if we fail, He is faithful and just to forgive us[95]. He is the one that said

---

94 Matthew 14:29.

95 "If we confess our sins, he is faithful and just and will forgive us our sins and purify us from all unrighteousness.", 1 John 1:9.

"seventy times seven"[96]. It doesn't matter what religion says; it doesn't even matter what we tell ourselves. If we decide today to listen to the voice of God, we can experience the extraordinary purpose He has for us.

Yet, we're also challenged to persevere. The dream in our hearts is often a lot more poetic and shiny than what we have in our hands today to do. However, it's only through today's effort and hard work that we will be positioned to reach our future dreams. Each season of our lives is essential, and the degree of faithfulness we attain in each season will establish and welcome the next. "His lord said to him, 'Well done, good and faithful servant; you were faithful over a few things, I will make you ruler over many things. Enter into the joy of your lord.'"[97] Let's not fall into the trap of trivialising and losing today to future dreams and plans. What has God placed in our hands today? Let's be faithful, and God will lead us to the next step.

A few months ago, I wrote a phrase on a piece of paper and stuck it to our fridge: "God moves, and we are moving with Him". That is, for me, a constant reminder that no matter what season we are living through, God

---

96 "Then Peter came to Him and said, 'Lord, how often shall my brother sin against me, and I forgive him? Up to seven times?' Jesus said to him, 'I do not say to you, up to seven times, but up to seventy times seven.'", Matthew 18:21-22 NKJV.

97 Matthew 25:21.

always has more. His thoughts are always higher than ours. So, therefore, let's work on what we have in front of us today, but in the constant expectation of what God will do next.

This is our time

Just like Esther lived her days out with purpose, you and I also have the opportunity to do the same. God has included us in His plan. He has been calling us for such a time as this. We were born for such a time as this; to give Him glory and serve people around us.

My prayer today is that we may have our eyes opened to heaven's perspective and that we see ourselves as God sees us. Just like God didn't let Esther down and didn't abandon her but favoured her instead, He won't let us down either, won't abandon us, and we will receive His favour.

FAITH TO GET MOVING

There isn't one person in history who has done something for God without going through a defining moment. These people's stories are distinguished by very tough choices. There's always a time when one has to choose between what God has said and what we want or think about something. I believe that faith is precisely our response in the face of events like this. In other words, our faith is demonstrated by our actions and not only in our thoughts and words.

I grew up listening to the stories of these faith heroes from ancient or recent times, who simply decided to let themselves be moved by the Holy Spirit of God, challenging everybody and everything, but mostly themselves.

During my youth, I was privileged to be part of one of these great movements of God upon the Earth, known as a revival. The windows of Heaven were opened over the city of Curitiba[98], and we saw "broken hearts making history", as Martin Smith[99] once sang prophetically. The Holy Spirit touched us and convicted our hearts to do something. Once timid and reluctant, the Church boldly witnessed and advanced, preaching the Gospel everywhere.

Services would last for hours and nobody wanted to go home because there was a powerful sense of God's presence at all times. Soon we started to hold two, then three services, and my family was often in all of them. I look back and remember my friends and colleagues, from our spiritual camps, and from moments of intense visitation from Heaven, and I see many of them today spread all over the world, spreading this fire and passion that started in those days.

We've heard many testimonies of what God was doing. People would dream of the address, wake up and go there to be saved. The biblical and ministry school took place in the prisons. People were miraculously healed. Transvestites and prostitutes were reached by the

---

98 TN: The capital city of the state of Parana, in Brazil.

99 *"We'll see broken hearts making history"*
History Maker © Furious? Records, by Martin Smith.

love of God. New evangelistic frontiers were opened, and the Church would actively preach in schools, hospitals, prisons, streets and everywhere, day or night. A true apostolic revival, with the restoration of the ministry gifts that Paul taught us about. The teaching I received back in those days formed the foundation of who I am today. The prophetic words I received gave me life and direction. The pastoral care sustained me and guarded me at every moment. Evangelism gave me mission and purpose.

One of the most significant moments happened to me during a conference when we were ministered to by pastor Claudio Freidzon from Argentina. Claudio and Betty Freidzon had been experiencing a supernatural revival in Buenos Aires for over thirty-five years. The parallels between what God did there and what He was doing in Brazil were extraordinary.

Those were days of an intense outpouring of God's presence. I served as a volunteer in the worship team, but I was a bit disappointed to see everybody else receiving from God, while it seemed as if nothing was happening to me.

In the last meeting of this conference, when Claudio Freidzon had already left, and only the pastors from our church were there, I was touched by God in an unexpected way. I remember falling to my face on the ground. I expected that God would speak to me through prophecy, but that was perhaps the first time in my life when I heard the Holy Spirit speaking directly to my heart.

His voice whispered a few words. Among other things, He said, "I'm going to take you far away, to England". I know He was the one who spoke. These words changed the course of my life. I don't believe I told this experience to anyone for several years.

Years later, newly married, my wife Lillian woke up one morning and told me a dream she had had. She said we were ministering in a church service and the presence of God was very intense. There were many people with white hair in the congregation. And she asked, "Where is this?" God answered, "It's in England".

I was stunned. I had never told Lillian what God had said to me before. She had never imagined before or even thought about going to England. From that moment on, we were sure that God had spoken to us and that He would lead us to that country. That happened in 2004 and we kept it close to our chests.

Of course, we also had our moments of weakness and doubt. When we told our dream to people, we were frequently discouraged, even by close friends and people we thought would understand and support us. People who know me will know that I like to solve problems. When a problem shows up, I say "challenge accepted" and press ahead.

So I started to study and investigate the requirements and what I could do from my end. After all, so many people move out of Brazil to live abroad. What I found out, though, is that there was no easy route for me. There was no clear path to European citizenship to explore. In addition, there was a global economic crisis developing, so any route that once allowed for spontaneous immigration was now closed. There was only one route left for me, the toughest of all: an employment sponsored visa.

Some, in my place, would have simply packed their suitcases and gone, thinking whatever will be, will be. I knew, however, that I couldn't just immigrate illegally because in doing that, I'd have no authority in the spiritual realm to do anything. The dream in our hearts was to see this same revival, this same move of God, touching the United Kingdom again, just like in the days of the Welsh Revival.

After some time, while experiencing a new wave of revival from Heaven and living in Ponta Grossa[100], my wife and I decided to believe. We decided to trust and believe, despite what others were saying or the impossible nature of the assignment. And while doing this, we had our defining moment. God taught us many things in

---

100 TN: A city in the state of Parana, in Brazil.

those days. He showed us that we needed to act and position ourselves in favour of what God had said.

Therefore, those years we spent in Ponta Grossa were a time of preparation, a time of spiritual preparation because we saw God move powerfully in those days. We learned that our weakness is nothing when we have a strong God. It was also a time to prepare academically and financially. We understood that getting ready in those areas was the same as having faith. We understood our actions were a live demonstration of what we really believed.

I remember a conversation I had with a couple, friends of ours, and they told us how God had spoken to them several years before that He would take them to preach the Gospel in the land of their ancestors, in Italy. They felt their heart burning for this calling. However, when I asked what they were doing about it, they said that they were not doing anything.

On that day, I encouraged them to believe. Belief is not demonstrated by positioning oneself against something but in favour of it. Faith is action. They needed to learn Italian and apply for Italian citizenship.

Our faith is the response we give to what God has said to us and the extraordinary is His response in return.

So, in the same way, my wife and I started working in response to what God had said so that when the extraordinary came, we would be ready for it. And God, indeed, performed the extraordinary. The route I thought was the hardest, impossible even, was the one God used to take us into that new season of our lives. In September 2014, God brought us to the United Kingdom. Like the psalmist once said, we could even say that "we were like those who dream"[101] because we had absolute certainty that the hand of God had done it.

We can't talk about faith here without talking about Abraham. He is our biblical reference where faith is concerned. James even cites him as our father in faith[102]. In the letter to the Romans, Paul calls Abraham the father of us all because of his faith[103].

About him, Paul also writes, "Against all hope, Abraham in hope believed and so became the father of many nations, just as it had been said to him, 'So shall your offspring be.' Without weakening in his faith, he faced

---

101 "When the Lord brought back the captivity of Zion, we were like those who dream. Then our mouth was filled with laughter, and our tongue with singing. Then they said among the nations, 'The Lord has done great things for them.'", Psalms 126:1-2 NKJV.

102 "Was not our father Abraham considered righteous for what he did when he offered his son Isaac on the altar?", James 2:21. NT: Some Portuguese translations of the Bible, in this verse, refer to Abraham as "our father in faith".

103 "Therefore, the promise comes by faith, so that it may be by grace and may be guaranteed to all Abraham's offspring – not only to those who are of the law but also to those who have the faith of Abraham. He is the father of us all.", Romans 4:16.

the fact that his body was as good as dead – since he was about a hundred years old – and that Sarah's womb was also dead. Yet he did not waver through unbelief regarding the promise of God, but was strengthened in his faith and gave glory to God, being fully persuaded that God had power to do what he had promised."[104]

We could say Abraham had a model faith, and this faith was marked by the actions he had in response to the words declared by God about him. So, if we want to learn what it's like to put our faith into practice, we should look at Abraham's example. The way Abraham reacted to the revelation and the promise of God is a practical demonstration of what faith is.

We have heard about faith in many different contexts and with many different implications. The world has its own opinion about the subject. Religious people also have their views about it. And what about us, the saved? More than anybody else, we really need to comprehend what faith is and, more importantly, put it into practice.

---

104 Romans 4:18-21.

Jesus once said we need to "have the faith of God"[105], which then challenges us not only to believe in Him but also to believe like Him and with Him. This revelation is deeper and implies that we can be participants in His purposes and His government. So, we can also declare that something will be done from a position of sure knowledge and it really will.

The Holy Spirit himself reveals in the scriptures that, without faith, it's impossible to please God, as we read in the book of Hebrews: "And without faith it is impossible to please God, because anyone who comes to him must believe that he exists and that he rewards those who earnestly seek him."[106].

So if you and I want to please God, we need to have a very clear perspective about this subject called faith. We can't simply relate to it based on our own ideas and traditions, as the world does, but we need the correct

---

105 "Jesus replied, "Let the faith of God be in you! Listen to the truth I speak to you: Whoever says to this mountain with great faith and does not doubt, 'Mountain, be lifted up and thrown into the midst of the sea,' and believes that what he says will happen, it will be done.", Mark 11.22-23 TPT.

Many English translations say "have faith in God", although many scholars suggest the more accurate translation is "have the faith of God" or "God-like faith".

NT: Apart from TPT, also CJB, DRA, GNV and RGT prefer "faith of God", over "faith in God".

106 Hebrews 11:6.

perspective. We need to comprehend, from God's perspective, what faith is.

If we look again at Paul's words, but in another translation, we read, "For he was past hope, yet in hope he trusted that he would indeed become a father to many nations, in keeping with what he had been told, 'So many will your seed be.' His trust did not waver when he considered his own body — which was as good as dead, since he was about a hundred years old — or when he considered that Sarah's womb was dead too. He did not, because of lack of trust, decide against God's promises. On the contrary, because he trusted he was given power as he gave glory to God. He was fully convinced that what God had promised he could also accomplish."[107]

Faith means trust

The first thing that grabs my attention when I read these verses in this translation is the translator's choice of words in replacing the word 'faith' with 'trust'. It can't get more straightforward than this because, in its simplest sense, faith means trust. To have faith is not a force or positive thinking, and it's not a denial of

---

107 Romans 4:18-21 CJB.

circumstances. To have faith is to take actions based on trust.

God, the most-high, the all-powerful, creator of the Earth and all the Universe turned his face to Abraham and said, "Your seed will be great, and your offspring". God told Abraham he would have many children, his offspring would be very numerous, and he would be the father of nations.

God Himself said it! This was no small, common, weak or powerless declaration, without strength or purpose. The voice of God is never without purpose. No! God had spoken!

The one thing Abraham most wanted in his life was to have children. Everything Abraham wanted was to have some offspring. He had tried many times and even lost all hope. God, then, comes and says he not only is going to have children but a countless crowd of them, like the sand of the sea, like the stars in the sky. God's dream was far more exceptional than Abraham's. Abraham's dream was already impossible in his sight. God's dream, then, might have seemed like insanity.

God speaks with Abraham and tells him His dream. Abraham, however, saw himself as the impotent man that he was, as good as dead. He was an older man who was unable to conceive children. His wife had been barren since her youth and furthermore, she was now an older woman whose womb was as good as dead.

He had all the reasons to laugh about it all and then forget about it. He had biology, logic, and his whole life experience as irrefutable evidence that it was impossible for him to have children. Yet, God seemed to ignore all that.

However, as we read, "His trust did not waver when he considered his own body (…) or when he considered that Sarah's womb was dead too."[108]. Abraham considered his situation. He looked at himself. He looked around and saw his wife. I believe the key here is that he didn't "waver". He didn't "only" consider these things.

We, just like Abraham, will also certainly look at ourselves, and our circumstances, and we will ponder about all the facts and, finally, see all the impossibilities. The problem comes when we decide to stop right there, in that place of doubt and decide we won't move because we've made up our minds that it would be impossible anyway, so there's no point doing anything.

Indeed, we use the most reasonable excuses and even convince ourselves that that's how things are and nothing can change them. We say we need to have both feet on the ground, that we need to be rational and analyse everything including our circumstances.

---

108 "His trust did not waver when he considered his own body —
which was as good as dead, since he was about a hundred years old
— or when he considered that Sarah's womb was dead too.",
Romans 4:19 CJB.

Undoubtedly, being rational is part of human nature. However, having faith in God and trusting Him, is deciding to be sure that something will happen, despite the circumstances, simply because God said.

The Bible affirms that whoever believes in the Lord Jesus and declares it with their mouth will be saved. Therefore, it's necessary to trust God for salvation. Based upon the circumstances, upon nature, we know that our body, our biological life, will end. But by faith, we know that He will raise us from the dead. We trust, then, that God will fulfil all that He has spoken.

The circumstances around us may present themselves as a health problem or a disease. They may also present themselves as a crisis or a financial need. They may come as unemployment or a physical or mental limitation, a global financial crisis or as a pandemic. You look at yourself, look around everywhere, and say, "This can't be happening." You consider your strength and, by realising you're weak, you might be tempted to stop.

The faith of God, though, challenges our circumstances and it's not an empty, void or unfounded challenge. On the contrary, faith is founded on something far superior to circumstances, something heavenly that made all that we can see: The word declared by God's mouth.

To have faith is to trust in what God said. It is to consider God's words more important than everything we can see. So Paul, inspired by the Holy Spirit, declares,

"By faith we understand that the universe was formed at God's command, so that what is seen was not made out of what was visible."[109]

Circumstances usually don't seem to agree with what God has said but God is not taken by surprise. As a matter of fact, the very mechanism God uses to transform our circumstances is His words. In other words, in His declaration there's the power to transform nothing into everything, darkness into light and dry bones into a great army[110]. There was darkness when God said, "let there be light", and everything was made new by His words. So, to have faith is to hang on to what God had said, despite the circumstances, with a sure conviction that they will not be able to resist God's words.

Faith means commitment

The second principle we can learn about faith from Abraham's life is that faith also means commitment. The narrative in the book of Genesis tells us, "No longer will you be called Abram; your name will be Abraham, for I have made you a father of many nations. I will make you very fruitful; I will make nations of you, and kings will

---

109 Hebrews 11:3.

110 Ezekiel 37.

come from you."[111] And, "God also said to Abraham, 'As for Sarai your wife, you are no longer to call her Sarai; her name will be Sarah. I will bless her and will surely give you a son by her. I will bless her so that she will be the mother of nations; kings of peoples will come from her.'"[112]

God didn't only promise something to Abram and Sarai, but He had given them new names. I've heard someone teaching about this change in Abram's name in the Hebrew language, demonstrating that God had taken one of the letters of His own name and included that in Abraham's as a symbol of His promise. Also, from that moment onwards, God also changed His own name, starting to refer to Himself as the God of Abraham.

Abram, which means "exalted father", had his name altered to Abraham, which means "father of a multitude". His new name represented his new role — he would be a father, but on a much larger scale, to bless every family on Earth. Sarai, which means "my princess", also had her name redefined for the new role she would play; she was now called "Sarah", which means "princess"; now without the possessive pronoun, her name would enlarge her scope of action, as she would now be the mother of kings and nations.

---

111 Genesis 17:5-6.

112 Genesis 17:15-16.

The meaning behind having a new name can be something extraordinary, but what would it have meant for Abram and Sarah back in their day?

Let's imagine the same thing happened to you today. In an incredible moment in the presence of God, God himself speaks to you and changes your name. In the face of such glorious revelation, how would you react? Maybe with joy and euphoria. And as you work out the meaning of your new name, you realise it aligns with everything you have ever dreamed about in your whole life. And God is the one saying this is so.

Then comes Monday. Would you be willing to tell everybody your name? Would you be willing to seek out the legal process to alter your name on your documents? What if this happened to us? Would we be willing to act upon the word God has declared?

Abraham and Sarah were not just new "prophetic names", which Abram and Sarai kept secret and private. Abram decided to commit to that divine revelation in a way that was much more intense they had initially imagined. They committed publicly to their new name in their secular life.

Was Abram prepared for the challenge? Was Sarai ready? Their attitude represented an extraordinary commitment but it was also extraordinarily compromising. Their reputation was at stake from that moment onwards.

Can you imagine what this meant? Maybe it was already embarrassing enough for Abram to have lived his whole life with a name like "exalted father". Now, a hundred years old, he would have to tell everybody that God had changed his name because he would be a father of a multitude. Indeed, people would have many questions, not about God's words but about Abram's mental health. They would think that the "old man Abram" had finally lost his mind.

People would say, "There goes Abram, (laughs)... wait, or is it still Abraham? ... (more laughs)... father of a multitude... can you imagine?! And Sarai... who now thinks she is Sarah! I think it's fine for people to believe in God and go to church, but this is fanaticism! These people need to keep their feet on the ground! Just imagine... somebody using 'spiritual revelation' as grounds for their actions?! They didn't have to tell everyone their new 'spiritual' names!"

Even though this is hypothetical, isn't it precisely what happens when we share what God has been saying to us with somebody else? Isn't it exactly what happens when we decide to believe that it's true? How often, do even those we trust give us a "cold shower", as the popular saying goes?

And because of negative experiences like these, sometimes, we Christians create a fictional wall of separation. We imagine that what happens at Church is our ecclesiastical or spiritual life, but what we do on the outside is secular or real life. So what happens in one, in the minds of most, must remain there; we think that "Christian life" is what will cheer me up and motivate me every Sunday, to give me the strength I need to live my days in the "real world" during the week.

When we look at Abraham's case, our role model of faith, we realise that to have faith is to commit; having faith is to make spiritual decisions that will affect our world. Having faith is to take the word of God as the "real world".

The vast majority of us are ready to waive our "spiritual life" in favour of our "secular life". But should it be this way? Should we really be willing to give up everything to favour our secular commitments? Should we be ready to adapt our spiritual life for it to agree with our worldly needs?

For some, changing church is just a matter of postal address. For others, going or not to a service depends on whether they are tired or not or maybe there's no better option, nothing more interesting to do. But should it really be this way? Should we allow compromises like that?

Or are we willing to modify our secular life according to what God has said?! For example, if God said, "stay in this place", and I decide to move away, just how important is God's word to me? Equally, if God says, "go to that other place", and I decide to stay, what is the importance of what He said?

Honestly, I believe that the difference between Abraham and most of us is not that we don't listen to God's voice, but maybe we just don't transform our world because of what God said. Abraham listened to the voice of God and decided to transform his world and commit wholeheartedly.

Once, while preaching, when trying to illustrate this aspect, I said: "To have faith is to act 'as if' what God said was true!". The absurdity of this sentence is that what He said is the truth, but why do we insist on acting as if it wasn't? To have faith is to give credit to God's voice and allow ourselves to make decisions based upon what He said. Faith means commitment!

Faith means speaking

The third principle we learn from Abraham's story is that faith involves speaking. Paul teaches us, "It is written: 'I believed; therefore I have spoken.' Since we have that same spirit of faith, we also believe and therefore speak"[113].

---

113 2 Corinthians 4:13.

Speaking is far more important than we might realise. We have been sharing until now about how much Abraham had trusted what God had said and how everything that God says is always full of purpose, meaning, and power. When God created the world, for example, it was by speaking that He released all of His creative power.

The narrative of Genesis says: "Now the earth was formless and empty, darkness was over the surface of the deep, and the Spirit of God was hovering over the waters. And God said, 'Let there be light,' and there was light."[114].

In the face of a formless and empty Earth and deep darkness, God simply "said," and everything was done. The Spirit of God was there which means the power of God was hovering over the waters, but this power only manifested into creative action when God used the device of speaking, of commanding, of words.

The Gospel of John tells us about the Word as the very person of Christ. Jesus is the Word of God made flesh, He is the living Word: "The Word became flesh and made his dwelling among us. We have seen his glory, the glory of the one and only Son, who came from the Father, full of grace and truth."[115].

---

114 Genesis 1:2-3.

115 John 1:14.

From the verses we read before, speaking is a direct consequence of believing. None of God's declarations was founded on uncertainty or doubt. Indeed, when creating the world, God made it by His words. His declaration was according to His own faith and His living Word produced creation through the power of the Holy Spirit.

Well, we are made according to God's own image and likeness. I heard a preacher once say we've been made according to the image and likeness of a God who created everything by speaking.

If we believe then some action is expected of us. One of the actions which is a direct consequence of believing, and one of the actions expected of us who believe, is speaking: "Then they asked him, 'What must we do to do the works God requires?' Jesus answered, 'The work of God is this: to believe in the one he has sent.'"[116]And if we believe, we also speak.

That's why God spares no effort to teach us about the power of the tongue so many times in scripture; because the declaration contains the very potential to activate the power of God by the Holy Spirit. This same power that was at work during the creation is at the disposal of us who believe, but it will only be set in motion by a declaration.

---

116 John 6:28-29.

There's a lot more to speaking than what we are able to comprehend. The enemy invests highly in filling our mouths with his thoughts so that our confessions and declarations are based on the precepts of this world. The third chapter from the book of James, for example, only talks about this: the need for us to rule our tongues. If it was a secondary matter, the enemy wouldn't invest so much to try and catch us in our words.

I believe there are heights we haven't yet reached in God, or we might be late or stuck somewhere, simply because of our lack of speaking.

When we declare, when we say words, we're sowing spiritually. We're planting the seed on higher ground for a higher harvest. Sometimes, we limit ourselves to thinking about God's things and reduce them with the filter of our own thoughts and ideas, but I challenge you to open your mouth and declare God's thoughts.

It's not always easy to declare what God has said, especially if our circumstances are not aligned to it. One of the most challenging experiences of our lives happened when my son, Nathan, got very ill when he was still three years old. By the grace of God, we lived less than a block from one of the main hospitals in our city at the time.

He had a high fever, and we decided to bathe him. But there, in the bath, he began to lose consciousness and roll his eyes. We got desperate, took him out of the tub, and ran to the hospital just as we were. My daughter, Louise, ran barefoot. She was only six years old when it happened, but she remembers that traumatic day only too well.

When we got into the hospital, I handed over my son to the emergency doctors, and stood still for a little, catching my breath. Then, I heard my daughter as she asked my wife: "Is Nathan going to die, Mom?" That was like a blow to my heart. However, my wife, moved by the Holy Spirit, said, "He is not going to die because God has said something different".

In fact, years before, when she was pregnant, my wife and I had been to Buenos Aires [117]and received a prophetic word from pastor Claudio Freidzon[118], who prayed for the child and said in Spanish, *"Grande predicador"*, which means, "great preacher". We believed that word, and our faith grew even in the middle of that hopeless situation, it was our foundation to walk through it.

What Nathan had on that day, we learned later, was an episode of seizure resulting from high fever, a problem which I had also had as a child. God had healed me then, and I was sure He would heal my son. We had put

---

117 NT: The capital city of Argentina.

118 NT: Senior Pastor at "Iglesia Rey de Reyes" (King of Kings Church), a Christian congregation in Buenos Aires.

our faith in action, then, when we decided to declare the words God had said. After that day, Nathan never had an episode like this again, and for God's glory, he's growing into a very happy, intelligent and healthy boy.

We are called to challenge circumstances with our faith, which is not a random denial or mindless idea but established on what God said! Even if it may sound crazy, the firmest foundation you have is what God has declared about you. For this reason, declare with your mouth what God has said over you; trigger into action this power of God in your life.

We've seen before how Abram had his name changed into Abraham, and in the same way, his wife Sarai had her name changed into Sarah. Each day, when they said their new names, they declared their faith in God.

Their names meant something fantastic and pointed towards their eternal purpose, that their offspring would be numerous. However, they still remained childless. But God was doing something new. He was declaring over them a new destiny and a new hope. The words God had said contained the power to produce something new. The invitation of God, then, was for Abram and Sarai to start prophesying their new names, declaring the words of the Lord in faith, in agreement and in trust.

Each time they told people not to call them by their old names, but by the new names instead, they were declaring their faith with their mouths and demonstrating their faith with action.

If we believe, we speak. If we believe, we open our mouths and declare the Word of God over us. With our declaration, we start a process of heavenly fruitfulness. Because of our authority over this creation, we put into motion the power of Heaven on the Earth. We are called to be partners of God in the transformation of circumstances around us when we use our mouths to declare the words He said.

When we speak, we trigger creative power into action, with the authority we have received from the heavenly places, and we govern the Earth. As it is written, "And God raised us up with Christ and seated us with him in the heavenly realms in Christ Jesus"[119].

Faith means decision

The fourth principle about faith we can see from the life of Abraham is that faith means decision. The Bible tells us that Abraham "did not by lack of trust decide

---

119 Ephesians 2:6.

against God's promises", but "by trust he was given power as he gave glory to God"[120].

While analysing Abraham's story, I see that he positioned himself with two attitudes that led him to live the entirety of what God had said. First, he didn't decide against God's promises.

It's very easy to decide against God's promises. All it takes is for us to look around or at ourselves. All it takes is for us to stop. Doing nothing is enough already. Whatever it is that God had said to you and me, if we look around, we're at the risk of saying, "This is impossible; it will never happen, not to me". If we use our mouths for these words, we actually produce the opposite of what we want.

As we said earlier, when God says something, it will indeed seem impossible at that moment. That doesn't move God, though, because his words are the very thing that transforms the impossible into reality.

His declared voice is the very release of God's power, the same power that performed creation itself, the same power that resurrected Jesus from the dead, that's the power released by the words spoken by God! The declaration from God is not made impossible by the circumstances,

---

120 "He did not by lack of trust decide against God's promises. On the contrary, by trust he was given power as he gave glory to God.", Romans 4:20 CJB.

but it contains the very power necessary to transform circumstances.

Abraham's second attitude was to decide in favour of God's promises. Abraham did that. How? By believing what God had said, he decided to take action for that promise to happen.

It's fascinating to see how the scripture says that he was given power as he gave glory to God. It means that Abraham had considered what God had said as done, complete, and finished. He believed so much that he even thanked God for it. He didn't use his mouth to keep on saying, "I can't, I'm unable to, I won't go". No! He didn't decide against it. He didn't stand against it. Instead, he used his mouth to thank God for what was going to happen.

Yet, we can see how giving glory to God is much more than simply saying how much we're grateful for. Giving glory to God is acting in such a way as to honour what God has said. It is to grant value to what God said. Therefore, when you and I walk according to the words declared by God, we give Him glory and honour.

So as Abraham did that, he was given strength. And as Abraham acted in such a way to glorify God for what He had said, he received the necessary power to transform his condition.

Abraham and Sarah were rejuvenated, literally. He didn't have physical vitality anymore. He was very elderly, more than a hundred years old and counting, already impotent, unable to have children. And so was Sarah. The power of God in their life produced the impossible. Although almost dead already, it was as if they were young again.

The strongest element in the Universe

If we turn our attention back to Jonah, we might find ourselves asking the following question: What had Jonah done wrong? He certainly believed what God had said was true. Jonah didn't have any doubts that God was speaking to Him. He knew that if he acted on it, God would bring the supernatural over the city of Nineveh. However, he decided to stand against the words declared by God. God had said: "Go to Nineveh"[121]. He, however, followed in the opposite direction and went to Tarshish[122]. The scripture tells us that he paid for the ticket. Rashi, a Jewish commentator from the Middle Ages, suggests that Jonah paid not only for his ticket but a fee equivalent to all the available seats on the ship, to ensure its immediate

---

121 Jonah 1:2.

122 Jonah 1:3.

departure[123]. This means that Jonah was so convinced in his rebellious decision making that he made a considerable investment in the opposite direction to God's instruction.

What we see in Jonah's story is the direct opposite of Abraham's story. Jonah was not a great hero of faith who had made an unshakable faith-based decision. Instead, he acted as any of us would. I take comfort in Jonah's erratic journey, which reminds us so much of our own. I take comfort in the fact that God decided to give him further chances, even when Jonah got it all wrong.

Jonah got it wrong, then right, then wrong again. In all this, God demonstrated great patience with him and was intent on not excluding Jonah from his plans.

Sometimes we listen to the words declared by God, and we believe that it's going to happen, but we continually move as if it wasn't true. God says something, and we believe it's true, but why do we still take our decisions in life as if those things were never going to happen?

As my wife and I served the Lord in Ponta Grossa, we had the chance to buy a house. It was an excellent opportunity, so we didn't let it pass. But, all of a sudden, we found ourselves in the middle of an unexpected situation. On the one hand, we had a dream in our hearts to obey God's voice and follow him to a foreign country. But, on the other hand, we were now owners of a house,

---

123 Rabbi Shlomo Yitzhaki is most known by the acronym Rashi.
Mentioned in: *"Go to Nineveh"*, Steven Bob, Pickwick Publications.

which would take all our resources to renovate to our taste.

People encouraged us to invest and renovate it, but, as time passed, the more problematic it became. Finally, we realised that we were chasing other people's dreams. We had made a significant investment in the opposite direction of where we were supposed to be going. When we understood that, eventually, we sold the house. Despite everything, God still allowed us the necessary profit from the sale to finance our coming to the United Kingdom.

It's time to take a stand based upon what God declares about us. It's time for us to believe, for real. It's time we trust and believe what God said about us is true. The difference between believing and trusting is found in what we do in response.

Trusting will undoubtedly lead me to make the right decisions, so the words declared by God actually happen. As Paul said, "Let God be true, and every human being a liar"[124]. Trusting is knowing God is the truth, and despite everything, the truth is what remains. So we need to

---

124 "Not at all! Let God be true, and every human being a liar. As it is written: 'So that you may be proved right when you speak and prevail when you judge.'" Romans 3:4.

decide, today, to stand with the strongest element of the Universe, the Word that comes from the mouth of God[125].

---

125 "Jesus answered, "It is written: 'Man shall not live on bread alone, but on every word that comes from the mouth of God.'" Matthew 4:4.

THE RIGHT TIME

I am part of the so-called generation Y (or millennials), which means I grew up in the decades of 1980 and 1990 and reached adulthood during the turn of the new millennium. It was an exciting time to be alive.

My brothers and I would play on "the street" every day. We would ride our bicycles, go alone here and there (to parks, playgrounds, mini-markets, etc.). We would go out of the house to play and only come back when we heard our mom yelling, calling us for lunch or dinner. We would ride cars with no seatbelts. On road trips, my brother and I would lie down and sleep across the back seat, each on one side.

Technology was extremely primitive when compared to today's standards. I remember the colossal tube televisions – black and white or in colour –, the first wireless telephones (measuring maybe 15 inches long and weighing more than a pound), VCRs with remote control; turntables, cassette players, walkmen and telephone booths everywhere.

At the same time, my generation saw the beginning of the technological revolution, which made the world what it is today. We saw the first gigantic mobile phones and lived through the first days of the dialled internet. We played video games on Atari, Sega Genesis and Super Nintendo, saw the first Macintosh computer and witnessed the race of the clocks for the *pentium* PCs.

In the last years of the nineties, technology was advancing very quickly. So quickly, indeed, that we thought we were going to see the extraordinary Marty McFly and Dr Emmet Brown visit using a time machine built in the *DeLorean* of the *Back to the Future* trilogy[126]. In that movie, Marty McFly travels 30 years into the future, to the 21st of October 2015, to help his son. The future, then, had all sorts of flying cars, holograms and *hoverboards* (basically floating skateboards). Eventually, the 21st of October 2015 came, but not the technological wonders we saw in the film.

---

126 *Back to the Future Part II*, 1989, directed by Robert Zemeckis and written by Bob Gale. © Universal Pictures.

That wasn't the only movie to explore the idea of time travel. It is indeed a subject that fascinates humanity and expands our imagination. What would we do if it was possible to travel to any other place in space and time? Which events from history would we want to witness? To where or when in the future would we like to go? What would we find there?

Certainly, the subject of time fascinates us, maybe because it is our final frontier, impossible to be tamed. There isn't a single person who can escape time. It doesn't matter how much we try. No matter what we do, time moves only in one direction, "forward". It's impossible to escape from it. Time moves and never stops. It will always catch us.

When I look back I realise, once again, how our lives move too fast, like a whisper even. It's like Bildad said to Job, "For we were born only yesterday and know nothing, and our days on earth are but a shadow."[127] In the little time we have on the Earth, you and I have dreams and projects to carry out and people to bless and influence. Also, we have the eternal purposes from God to draw out[128].

---

127 Job 8:9.

128 "The purposes of a person's heart are deep waters, but one who has insight draws them out." Proverbs 20:5.

From this perspective, in our eyes, time can be a tormentor. It seems to move too quickly for some things, but when we have great expectations, it seems like it doesn't move at all. While living in the context of evangelical Christianity, there will always be someone to tell us, "It's not in your time, but in God's time". That might seem splendid for the person saying it, but it's not necessarily comforting for the one on the receiving end.

If someone says something will happen "in God's time", we usually think it will be an extremely long time. So we think of how God is in the heavens and lives in eternity. One day for Him is like a thousand years, and a thousand years is like a day, so it all seems like it will take an eternity to happen.

I believe the source of our anxiety regarding this subject, "time", is that we don't comprehend how God sees time. We could say our perspective about this matter is limited or even short-sighted. Jesus himself says, "You are in error because you do not know the Scriptures or the power of God!"[129]

As we said before, our time is finite and limited; it can't be stopped and will always catch up with us. Therefore, while we can give ourselves the luxury of not understanding many things, we cannot afford not to understand time. Of course, we can deceive ourselves

---

129 Matthew 22:29.

and make mistakes about many things, but if we make a mistake and deceive ourselves about time, the cost will be too high.

We all know time is a limited resource. We also know how to measure time and we learn that very early. We all know what the world thinks about time. You've certainly heard phrases like: "time is money" or "live each moment as if it was your last," or "you only get one life", among others.

All these ideas are recorded in our hearts and minds, leading us sometimes to have a distorted vision of the subject. And if we have a distorted or incomplete image, we will also regard time in a distorted and incomplete way.

Without the proper instruction, we are at the risk of regarding the subject of time in a "childish" way. A child doesn't have the same perception of time as an adult has. Children think that time is irrelevant and imagine it should always be at their service. The first sign of maturity, though, is to realise that things around us don't only exist to serve us.

I want to invite you to walk with me through the scriptures to comprehend what time means for God. Then we'll no longer be shortsighted about the matter, remaining in the dark where time is concerned, we'll have clarity and complete revelation. Finally, I want to share what I have learned from the Holy Spirit about this subject.

How the Bible describes the time

First and foremost, we will begin by building our foundation exclusively upon what the Word of God says about time. Our perspective about time comes from referencing what we can measure and calculate. This means that, for us, time is what we experience in the passing of minutes, hours, days and years. The Bible, though, in both old and new testaments, uses three words, or even three distinct constructs which have been translated to us as the idea of time.

The first of these concepts is found in the scriptures in the Greek word "*aeon*" (or in its equivalent in Hebrew, "*ad*"). It means an indefinite moment of time, indicating the notion of eternity, the absence of end, or even the absence of time itself.

The prophet Isaiah, for example, writes that God "inhabits eternity"[130], which is the same as saying, He

---

130 "For thus says the High and Lofty One who inhabits eternity, whose name is Holy: "I dwell in the high and holy place, with him who has a contrite and humble spirit, to revive the spirit of the humble, and to revive the heart of the contrite ones.", Isaiah 57:15 NKJV.

inhabits *"aeon"*, this place above time. John, in his Gospel, also mentions the words of Jesus: "For God so loved the world that he gave his one and only Son, that whoever believes in him shall not perish but have eternal life."[131] Therefore, the life we receive is of this same quality – *"aeon"*, endless, eternal.

The second concept is found in the Greek word *"chronos"* (or in its equivalent in Hebrew, *"zeman"*). It means the quantity of time, the space or interval of time, the duration, the order, the sequence or succession of events, a time that is specifiable, quantifiable, measurable. This is the concept we are most familiar with, and it's the principle that rules over our natural world.

In the Gospel of Mark, we see how, on the occasion of Jesus' birth, "Herod called the Magi secretly and found out from them the exact time the star had appeared"[132]. There was an exact *"chronos"*, the specific year, month, day, hour, minute and second. In his Gospel, Luke tells us how on the occasion of Jesus' temptation, the devil took him to a high place and then "showed him in an instant all the kingdoms of the world"[133]. Once again, in an exact moment, a specific instant, a determined *"chronos"*.

---

131 John 3:16.

132 Matthew 2:7.

133 Luke 4:5.

Finally, the third concept found in the scriptures is in the Greek word "*kairos*" (or in its equivalent in Hebrew, "*eth*"). It refers to a quality of the time or season, a period characterised by certain events, a favourable time, a time of opportunity, a fortuitous time, appropriate, the right season.

Paul writes to the Romans that, "at the right time, while we were still helpless, Christ died for ungodly people"[134]. This is actually saying, within a "*kairos*", in the appropriate season, or when a window of opportunity had opened. He also writes to the Galatians, saying that we must work good to everyone, "whilst we have time"[135]. This means, while there is "*kairos*", or while we can do it, or while the season is appropriate for it.

For example, let's see how the most classic Bible verse about time is constructed: "There is a time for everything, and a season for every activity under the heavens"[136]. Well, here we have two of these concepts together in the same verse. Firstly, when the author says "there is a time", he is saying, "there is '*chronos*'", which means, there's a day in the calendar, a time on the clock,

---

134 Romans 5:6 GW.

135 "Therefore, whilst we have time, let us work good to all men, but especially to those who are of the household of the faith", Galatians 6:10 DRA.

136 Ecclesiastes 3:1.

in which all things will happen. But the author also says "a season for every activity", which means there is "*kairos*", the right time, the appropriate season for all activities, plans and intentions.

These apparently minor variations are essential for comprehending what the scripture is really saying. If we go quickly through these concepts, I know they might seem confusing and complex, but with the grace of God, allow me to try and make this image a bit clearer. When we see and understand this clearly, we will be able to revolutionise the way we relate to time.

In our evangelical tradition, we're accustomed to the fact that "*chronos*" is our time and that "*kairos*" is God's time. But, from what we just exposed, can you see how much this thought is incorrect and incomplete? To begin with, there are three dimensions of time and not two. And the meaning of each of these is amplified in conjunction with the other two.

The "eternal" time ("*aeon*") is the time God inhabits. It's a place out of time as we know it, or better, above all time. For God, past, present and future are all before him. He lives in eternity, in this place, and there is also the place He invites us to inhabit. When God looks at us, he sees the whole of our lives. Indeed, He has placed his dreams and purposes for us in our hearts and He visualises all our days. The life He gave us in Christ is of this same quality and it originated in eternity; therefore, we will also be there with Him in eternity.

The "opportune" time, "*kairos*", is defined by appropriate seasons. As we read earlier, there's a right moment, a window of time specified for all plans. Also, there's a "chronological" time for everything. So the consolidation of these plans is performed in a specific moment in time, a particular "*chronos*".

There's something demarcated since eternity, from "*aeon*". What God established and specified since the beginning of time is presented for us in the form of appropriate seasons, "*kairos*", in which such purposes and intents can be accomplished. Moreover, there's also the exact time, "*chronos*", where we really achieve these projects and dreams.

The time and us

I remember the joy and expectation my wife and I had waiting for the birth of both of our children. We have two children, Louise and Nathan, born almost exactly three years apart. When babies are still in the womb, all parents imagine and dream about so many things. They think of what the child will look like, or what their personality will be like. They think of what they will achieve in life and what their dreams and expectations will be. They prepare the best they can to receive that new life.

A child comes to the world as a defenceless baby, totally dependent on their parents. After this, there is an immense amount of work and worry so that everything is perfect for that child. We feed, change, teach the first words, discipline, and love them.

But, the time for being a baby is short, and it passes very quickly. Soon the child will want to take their first steps, and as soon as they learn how to walk, they also learn how to run. The dynamics of this second phase are also very intense but very different from the first.

The child grows and develops. Each new phase presents different characteristics but also additional challenges. While the child grows, there will be challenges of many orders, like health, safety, and intellectual development. There will also be challenges regarding the teaching of principles and values so that they can always decide on the right path. There will always be new things, problems, challenges and worries until they reach adulthood and are ready to start their own journey in life.

Looking back, I miss the baby phase and early childhood, and part of me would like very much to revisit those days. However, even greater within me is the desire to see my children live a fulfilled life in each phase they are in.

No mom or dad would like their children to remain as babies beyond the determined time. It's healthy to be a baby for a particular season, but going past that season and staying a baby is not natural or healthy. So, there is a correct season (a *"kairos"*) for a child to be a baby, and then they can move from that season to the next. The greatest joy of a mom or a dad is seeing their children grow to become better than them, advance further than they ever did, and achieve higher than they ever will. The joy is robbed from us when these phases become abnormal and prolonged.

Therefore, there are specific *"kairos"*, specific seasons for us to be babies, children, teenagers, and, finally, youth and adults. There is also an appropriate season for us to be parents. There is a season in which we are biologically able to have children. This period has a beginning but it also has an end. As we know, there is a point when our bodies cease to be able to reproduce. The *"kairos"* is the season, the appropriate time, the right time for something to happen.

When I take the necessary steps for that to really happen, that is, with actions, only then will I be able to make that dream come to pass in a specific moment or date, a *"chronos"*. While I might be in the correct season, biologically speaking, to have children, I will only be able to actually have children if I take the necessary steps for that to happen: courtship, marriage, and marital relationship. Suppose all these steps happen in the appropriate season (the "*kairos*") then we will be the ones to determine what the exact "*chronos*" will be, ie. the exact date.

So, whenever there is an appropriate season, a suitable time, the primary influencer for the materialisation of that dream on a specific date is me. This way, **my will is the first factor to influence when the time of God is fulfilled in my life**.

Note that I'm not saying we should ignore the processes of God in our lives. On the contrary, it's often necessary that we live through specific experiences and wait for the right time, the opportune season, to finally come. Yet, as soon as this season of opportunity comes, it's up to us to take the necessary actions to bring that purpose to life. And in this sense, yes, our will is the core factor.

Let us remember Jonah once more. He heard the voice of God calling him to go to Nineveh[137]. While the opportune time was there before him, Jonah's will was not aligned with what God had said. Jonah had other priorities and more important things to do. Not being willing to go, he went the other way. If his will was aligned to God's voice, he could have gone and performed that mission with no major incidents. Jonah's

---

137 "The word of the Lord came to Jonah son of Amittai: 2 'Go to the great city of Nineveh and preach against it, because its wickedness has come up before me.'", Jonah 1:1-2.

story, happily for us, follows this tortuous path for our example so that we can learn and decide to align our will to God's voice.

Many of us go through similar experiences to Jonah. God speaks to us and our opportunity is right there. As we said before, the very declaration from God contains all the power to transform circumstances. So, if we align our will to what God has said, you and I will see the will of God taking place.

Just like with Jonah, sometimes we may not agree or want our mission. Sometimes, though, we might not feel qualified for it or feel weak and incapable. Jonah had also been in a place like this, in the belly of a fish and virtually dead, and he never thought God would include him in His plans again. But even there, in that impossible situation, Jonah found grace and favour, and again the season of opportunity was open.

We know the rest of the story and how Jonah bent his own will and followed in the right direction, even though he didn't entirely agree with the mission. So, even if Jonah was the wrong candidate for the job, according to our standards, Jonah's weaknesses and limitations didn't hinder God's greater purpose of saving that city.

One thing I've learned: you and I will never be the right person for the job, in our own eyes. In reality, if we feel like a perfect fit for the mission, we might still be missing some process of God to happen in our lives. I believe that, if we acknowledge our inadequacy and set foot out of our comfort zone, in our weakness, we will see the power of God in perfect action. And that's also what the apostle Paul teaches us: "But he said to me, 'My grace is sufficient for you, for my power is made perfect in weakness.' Therefore I will boast all the more gladly about my weaknesses, so that Christ's power may rest on me."[138]

Throughout my life, being by nature a reserved person, I was horrified at the idea of evangelism, and to be honest, I still am. So, when God called me to work in this very ministry, I was shocked because I have resisted it all my life. So, my will was always against it. There was a time of opportunity before me, but time after time, my own choices would lead me away.

I still remember the first time I took a risk and, in doing so, overcame my own will. After a Saturday night service, the youth group was going to the town to evangelise, and I decided to join them. Completely out of my comfort zone, I decided to follow the youth pastor closely, "only to observe", as I told myself. Before I realised what was happening, I was speaking and giving my testimony.

---

138 2 Corinthians 12:9.

We saw so many lives saved that night. Some of our group were playing the guitar and singing worship songs. People open-heartedly received the message of the Gospel and many of those who received Christ stayed there until the end. Some listened, others sang or cried, and some even danced. God's presence was powerful. The joy in my heart was overflowing. I looked at myself and was sure I couldn't do have done any of it, but I saw God in action when I didn't allow my own will to interfere.

And that's really the critical point. The will of our hearts will not always be in favour of what we're called to do. But, it's up to you and me to overpower our will with our decisions.

The will of God is eternal and comes from eternity. God's thoughts are way higher than ours[139] and originate from the *"aeon"*. God establishes a *"kairos"* for each stage of our lives and it's these seasons, these *"kairos"*, that present themselves as times of opportunity for us to fulfil each step of the journey that takes us to our destiny, our purpose on Earth.

Before us is a time of opportunity. However, in each season, or *"kairos"* opportunity, it is our prerogative to

---

139 "'For my thoughts are not your thoughts, neither are your ways my ways, declares the Lord. 'As the heavens are higher than the earth, so are my ways higher than your ways and my thoughts than your thoughts.", Isaiah. 55:8-9.

choose or determine the exact "*chronos*" of when it is going to happen. Therefore, at each season, the decision will always be ours. This way, **the second factor to influence when the time of God is fulfilled in our lives is our own decisions**.

We can see how our natural life demonstrates this. Even if somebody is at the right biological age to have children, it doesn't necessarily mean that they will have children. Many couples decide not to have children. So, even while there is an appropriate season, a "*kairos*", there won't be a specific time, a "*chronos*", because of their will and decisions.

Decision is not the same as will. As we said, I can make a decision even against my will, and this is called surrender. God says many things to us, and we will decide whether we want to do them or not. But my submission, the surrendering of my will, while choosing to obey the voice of God, will bring the effective time closer. Even if it means surrendering our will, our decisions can help determine the specific time for God's plans to be established. Therefore, the sooner we decide, the sooner we surrender, the sooner the time of God will be fulfilled in our lives.

The prophet Jonah is, once again, an excellent example. The will of Jonah was absolutely contrary to what God had asked him to do. And for a while, Jonah had kept his decision aligned only to his own desires. So,

Jonah invested time, resources, and all he had into following his own will in the opposite direction to what God had commissioned him to do.

It was only when Jonah decided to completely surrender, while still not fully agreeing, that he could really see the mighty hand of God in action through him. And as a result, that whole town was spared from destruction. Jonah is the example of someone who, in the appropriate season, within the *"kairos"* determined by God, got delayed, changing the exact time or *"chronos"* of it all happening. God's mercy and goodness are on display here. God didn't exclude Jonah from his plans for being "delayed". Yet, He continued to give Jonah opportunities to see the purpose of God fulfilled in his life.

Jesus came to this world when the "fullness of the time had come", as Paul writes to the Galatians: "But when the fullness of the time had come, God sent forth His Son, born of a woman, born under the law, to redeem those who were under the law, that we might receive adoption as sons."[140]

When the scripture talks about the "fullness of the time", the word here used in the original manuscripts is once again *"chronos"*. There was an appropriate season, a *"kairos"* determined by God for Jesus to be born, but Jesus, did even better and satisfied the exact *"chronos"*.

---

140 Galatians 4:4-5 NKJV.

The fullness of the time refers to the perfect use of the opportunity, which means Jesus didn't arrive late or lose any time. As soon as "*kairos*" began, He also made it His "*chronos*".

The majority of us have a wrong perspective about the subject time. So many tend just to keep waiting for the right time to arrive, and we do so in a completely passive manner. But if God declared a word to us, if He determined an opportune season, a "*kairos*", it's up to us to decide and make it happen within a "*chronos*" in our lives. So, it's up to us to bring it to reality and make sure the specific time arrives. We can't skip stages, and God is certainly the Lord of all time. However, the amount of time, the "*chronos*", we will spend in each season, "*kairos*", depends exclusively on us.

Our Christian life is, indeed, marked by different seasons. There is a first season when our lives begin. That's when we are born again through the faith that comes from the Gospel. In this season, as in our natural lives, we are like spiritual babies, which need to feed on milk[141]. Soon, the baby grows and learns to eat, walk and talk. This season of the beginning of our Christian life is tremendous, but we're not supposed to stop there. The purpose of God is for us to grow and not that we stay as a baby for years and years.

---

141 "Anyone who lives on milk, being still an infant, is not acquainted with the teaching about righteousness.", Hebrews 5:13.

The purpose of all living beings is to grow and multiply. And God wants us, as his children born from the Spirit, to fulfil this purpose and reach maturity. Indeed, **the third factor that will influence when the time of God is fulfilled in our lives is maturity**.

There is something higher for all of us. There's a higher and better purpose than just receiving spiritual milk from God. We will only be complete when we start living in the place God has prepared for us to live, a place of maturity, multiplication, and fruitfulness.

You and I need to decide to move forward and to grow up. However, the next season might not seem the most pleasant since it comes with new responsibilities. Not only merely receiving life, but also giving life, which is the highest purpose of human beings, making us more like our Heavenly Father.

Children focus only on themselves. Young people also think selfishly about their own values and goals. However, when we give life and become parents, we learn to put our children's interests above our own.

Moreover, multiplication itself is not the final goal. If we look at the example of the fruit trees, each fruit produced is also rich in seeds to produce new trees. Therefore, our mission is not only to save lives. It's necessary for every born again person to also grow and align with God's direction and purpose. It's essential to give each person the conditions needed for them to multiply.

Suppose we become a Church that only saves lives, bringing everyone in, growing in numbers. Will we be accomplishing the purpose designed by God? I would say not. Or at least, only incompletely. The purpose of God is for us to go forward and dedicate ourselves so that other people also become like leafy trees that can produce many fruits and multiply God's life.

There's a "*kairos*" in each season of our lives which is established and ordained by God. But, the time it takes to become real and materialise, the amount of "*chronos*" is determined by our will, decisions and maturity. Furthermore, the next season can only happen when the previous season finishes. Whether that time will be one day, one year, ten years, twenty years, fifty years, or never happens at all, depends exclusively on you and me.

I've heard it said, "The blame is mine, so I can give it to anyone I chose". Indeed, we can blame whoever or whatever we want for not taking some of the necessary steps in our journey. We can blame the pandemic, the government, the country's finances. We can blame *Brexit*[142], our jobs, bank accounts, pastors, spouses, children and, finally, even blame ourselves. But, the truth is, only when we decide to agree with God's voice and

---

142 *Brexit* is an acronym for "*Britain Exit*", which refers to the withdrawal of the United Kingdom from the European Union, which consolidated in the transition between 2020 and 2021. The event, of very great repercussion, was marked by crisis, uncertainty and speculations.

move in its direction will we create the conditions needed to unify our "*chronos*" and the "*kairos*" established by Him.

While "*chronos*" is measured in years, days, hours, minutes and seconds, "*kairos*" is measured in pre-conditions. Such pre-conditions can also be external. Let's see, for example, this scripture: "In the fourth generation your descendants will come back here, for the sin of the Amorites has not yet reached its full measure."[143]. This verse shows us that external factors may also determine the time or the appropriate season.

It was necessary to wait for the Amorites' sin to grow even bigger before God could declare judgment on that people at the hand of the nation of Israel. But, even then, when the time was finally decreed, "*kairos*" established, the opportune time for that nation to advance and conquer their inheritance, God's people settled for wandering in the desert. They decided to believe in bad news instead of what God had said. Now, today we hold a baton in our hands. This is our generation. This is our turn. What will our choice be? We are on the verge of a glorious time of opportunity, and it's up to us to decide to listen to God's voice and move forward.

---

143 Genesis 15:16.

The "*kairos*" of Grace

The coming of Jesus started a time of grace. It created a season in which salvation was put within the reach of anyone who believes. Jesus declared that "the time has come"[144]; in another translation, "the time is fulfilled"[145]. Once again, the word used in this scripture is "*kairos*". There is a time of opportunity established by God, and we're already in it.

We are living a time of salvation, an appropriate season for all humanity to receive the good news of the Gospel. What God declares about the time we're living today is precious, glorious, sublime, high, heavenly and eternal. "'The Spirit of the Lord is on me, because he has anointed me to proclaim good news to the poor. He has sent me to proclaim freedom for the prisoners and recovery of sight for the blind, to set the oppressed free, to proclaim the year of the Lord's favour.'"[146]

Before Christ, humanity had to wait for the One who would proclaim the grace and the Favour of the Lord, the Year of Jubilee. Now, when the opportune time had

---

144 "'The time has come,' he said. 'The kingdom of God has come near. Repent and believe the good news!'", Mark 1:15.

145 "and saying, 'The time is fulfilled, and the kingdom of God is at hand. Repent, and believe in the gospel'.", Mark 1:15 NKJV.

146 Luke 4:18-19.

come, Christ established a season, a *"kairos"*, in which we will all have access to this grace. It's up to you and me to live, access, and extend this grace to others in this time called "today".

Paul writes that "Creation waits in eager expectation for the children of God to be revealed"[147]. It's fascinating how, when we look at the original manuscripts, the Greek word used when Paul said "children" was the word *"huios"*. This word means nothing but a son who has already achieved maturity, a son ready to fulfil his purpose, ready for fruitfulness. And like we said before, our maturity is one factor that affects the fulfilment of the times of God, along with our will and decisions.

When God sent the plague of frogs over Egypt, the people were in great affliction. I can imagine how they weren't able to sleep for a few nights as frogs were everywhere, even in their bedrooms and beds. It got so bad that even the pharaoh decided to call Moses for him to pray to send the frogs away. Moses asked the pharaoh when he wanted that to happen and pharaoh surprisingly

---

147 Romans 8:19.

answered "tomorrow"[148]. In other words, it was up to him to choose when he would be free, and he decided to spend yet another night with the frogs.

Pharaoh was the only one who could decide when liberation would come to his house. In the same way, we are the only ones who can influence the time for the promises of God to come. In the pharaoh's case, there was already a solution, deliverance was available from God. But, even then, the pharaoh decided to leave it for one more night.

To us it seems like a very stupid decision indeed. In reality, however, many of us often do the same. We are doing it when we decide to 'leave for tomorrow', what God has decreed over us today, for whatever reason. In the pharaoh's case, it was probably his arrogance. In our case, many times, we may simply not know what God had said, or even we may not discern the time we're living in now.

---

148 "Pharaoh summoned Moses and Aaron and said, 'Pray to the Lord to take the frogs away from me and my people, and I will let your people go to offer sacrifices to the Lord.' Moses said to Pharaoh, 'I leave to you the honour of setting the time for me to pray for you and your officials and your people that you and your houses may be rid of the frogs, except for those that remain in the Nile.' 'Tomorrow,' Pharaoh said. Moses replied, 'It will be as you say, so that you may know there is no one like the Lord our God. The frogs will leave you and your houses, your officials and your people; they will remain only in the Nile.'", Exodus 8:8-11.

In this sense, the time of God for our generation is today. Today is the day of salvation, deliverance and healing. The word declared by God leaves no room for doubt about it. So we don't need to wait for tomorrow.

Sometimes we may think we don't deserve what God declared about us or that we may have failed so many times that our credit with Him is insufficient. Well, Jonah's story, reassures us that God is not astonished by our failures. Instead, He is the source of the strength we need to stand up again and move forward. So we live in this season, a *"kairos"* of the grace of the Lord, which is given to us.

The *"kairos"* of God's call

There are many callings and ministries buried and dormant for many reasons. Many of us encounter frustration and disillusionment along the way. We get let down by people, or even by ourselves. Sometimes we will feel weak, discouraged, incapable and unworthy. Some of us think we have lost all our chances or we might have failed dismally. Some just let time go by, passively waiting for things to happen in some distant future.

The day which is today, though, can be the day of our revolution. Today can be the day of our awakening because this is the time of God for our lives. We can decide today that we won't lose any more time. While we're still alive, God hasn't given up on us. Remember Abraham, that even while seeing himself as too old, half dead even, he decided to take action on the word that he had heard from the mouth of God. This same word had all the necessary power in itself to rewrite circumstances.

Today can be the best day of our lives. If we only decide to surrender, take the necessary steps, and subdue our own will. If we only get out of our comfort zone and follow God's voice. Then we will be able to see the fulfilment of everything God had said about us and this generation. I remember when we were still in Ponta Grossa, waiting for a promise of God. We waited for the fulfilment of the dream we had received from Him that He would take us to the United Kingdom. The dream was persistent and it burned in our hearts every day. We believed that God was leading us in everything.

In every experience, everything we went through and each project we worked on, I saw God acting supernaturally and extraordinarily on the things I couldn't do myself. We were there, helping in the ministry, making ourselves available to do what the Holy Spirit showed us. God, then, did what only He could do. We saw hundreds of people saved during evangelism and social justice events. We saw the Church experiencing the joy of participating in the beautiful work of saving souls. We witnessed a new Church being born in the town of Carambeí. We saw brothers and sisters waking and walking into their place of purpose. We saw the hunger and thirst in the hearts of many crying out for a revival from Heaven. We were forever changed by a visitation from a God that answers prayers.

There had come a point when we understood that the time had come. Not many people around us saw it, but it was evident in our hearts, even despite all the apparent impossibilities. In the first six months after we were aware of this change of season, I remember we were still trying to leave it to one side and move on.

Until a time came when we couldn't ignore it anymore, and, in March of that year, 2014, my wife and I agreed it was time and started taking the necessary actions. We began working with what we had in our hands, preparing CVs, doing research, taking tests, obtaining certificates and translating documents. Little by little, we were getting things ready on our end and when the miracle we were waiting for from God happened, we would be ready to go.

Then, the improbable, almost impossible, happened. Anyone who knows the United Kingdom's job market will know that it's extremely rare to find companies that will sponsor a visa. It was even more difficult while the United Kingdom was still part of the European Union. Even if we had found such a company, it was even more unlikely that they would offer a sponsorship for an overseas candidate. What happened to us was a miracle. On the 26th of September 2014, we landed in the United Kingdom. This day marked the beginning of a new season that God had prepared us for our entire lives.

When we decided to agree with God and move into action, knowing that what He had said was true, we were able to see His purposes fulfilled in our lives. The word He declared contained the power necessary to transform circumstances. It's up to you and me to decide to believe and then walk into what God has said, and it's up to him to do the impossible, which only He can do.

Today, my prayer is that we surrender ourselves and decide to follow His voice. I pray that we may be partners with God to make all the purposes He declared over us reality. I pray that we may be agents of salvation and bring the government of God over this generation.

AFTERWORD

Back in the 1960s, the famous Israeli archaeologist Professor Yigal Yadin[149] discovered thousands of date seeds buried under rubble during his excavations of Masada. Other date seeds were found in caves near the Dead Sea, from where also the famous biblical manuscripts came. A test revealed that those seeds were approximately two thousand years old.

They were, obviously, completely dry and lifeless, as they had been buried for two millennia. So, they were

---

[149] No Camels - Israeli Innovation News; https://nocamels.com/2020/09/2000-ancient-judean-dates-israeli-scientists/; acessado em 19/9/2021.

catalogued, stored, and there they stayed for the next forty years.

Two Israeli scientists[150], however, dared to try the improbable. They decided to plant the seeds and were actually able to get seven of them to germinate. They named each tree. The first of them was called Methuselah, in honour of the man who lived the longest on the Earth.

In September of 2020, the scientific community was shocked by the news that those trees had grown and produced fruits. The first harvest produced a total of one hundred and eleven dates of a unique kind, not known to our generation, but like those Jesus himself would have eaten when living in that region.

Historians of old, like Herodotus and Flavius Josephus, wrote about the excellent quality of these dates from Judea. It's said that even Herod used to present them to the emperor every year.

For about two thousand years, those seeds were there, dormant. They contained in themselves an enormous potential. They held the potential of a great tree that would produce the most excellent fruits, but they couldn't produce anything while they stayed there, buried under rubble.

---

150 Dra. Sarah Sallon e Dra. Elaine Solowey.
Haaretz - Israel News; https://www.haaretz.com/israel-news/.premium-2-000-year-old-seeds-produce-ripe-dates-in-israel-s-southern-arava-1.9152766, acessado em 19/9/2021.

It's the same with the purposes of God in our lives. There's a great potential deposited within us. We have within us the ability to produce many fruits and multiply the life we've received. If we just leave that potential buried under rubble, though, nothing will happen.

Today, I believe it's your challenge and mine to wake up and not let our purpose be lost in vain. Let us be like those seeds, producing many fruits to everybody's amazement. We may even think our time has passed and there's no more hope for us, but if there's hope for the tree that was cut down[151], there's also hope for us.

My prayer is that you and I will flourish into fruitfulness in the purpose He has called us for and that we have the assurance of the one thing that remains firm and unshakable: the word declared by the mouth of God. As it is written, "Man shall not live on bread alone, but on every word that comes from the mouth of God"[152].

In the face of many hardships and trials, beliefs, philosophies and contrary opinions, I want to encourage you to remember our life doesn't depend on any of that.

---

151 "For there is hope for a tree, if it is cut down, that it will sprout again, and that its tender shoots will not cease. Though its root may grow old in the earth, and its stump may die in the ground, Yet at the scent of water it will bud and bring forth branches like a plant.", Job 14:7-9 NKJV.

152 Matthew 4:4.

Instead, our life is established on every word that comes from the mouth of God.

Our life is in a safe place, a heavenly place. We have our feet on very solid ground in the words God has declared. Everything changes when we dare to live and walk in this place. We are challenged to dare to leave our apparently comfortable position and get moving today in the direction of the purposes of God for our life.

I pray that no weakness, tiredness or overload, no distractions or discouragement, no failures or defeat, and nothing else of this world may stand between us and what God has declared about us. I pray that we may be aware that while we're not moving, we're not giving life; while we're not moving, the world remains under slavery.

He calls us to get out of our hiding places. He calls us for such a time as this. My prayer is that we may decide today to hear and respond to this calling.

Acknowledgements

A book is not written alone. Indeed, it would be impossible for this book to reach you without the help of a good number of people, who, either directly or indirectly, have supported in the technical aspects, content, friendship, love and life. Many are directly responsible for the fact that I'm standing today, and I am grateful to them with my life.

In this sense, first, I would like to thank my wife, Lillian, my anchor in life and ministry. I don't know what I would do without you. I also thank my children, Louise and Nathan. They are also our ministry partners, living every joy and trial with us. Let God increase your reward greatly. I also thank my parents, Tirso and Vera, for their love and dedication and the great example and inspiration they are to me. I'm also grateful for our pastors, Robbie and Donna Howells, for their amazing support, for believing in us and for their passion and faithfulness to see the Kingdom of God advancing. May God take you to new heights every day.

Finally, I thank all pastors and leaders we've had throughout our journey in faith. I also thank those who stubbornly didn't give up on us when we wandered in our path. I also thank all of those who were part of our journey in friendship and prayers. This page would undoubtedly be too short if I were to mention all their names. We have, most definitely, a debt of love to all of you.

Saulo Santos

About the author

Saulo Oliveira Santos serves the Lord in the United Kingdom together with his family. He's been married to Lillian Matoso Santos since 2004; they have two children, Louise and Nathan, and currently live in Cardiff, Wales. They serve as associate pastors at The Warehouse Church. His passion and vocation is to inspire the Church to stand and fulfil their purpose in their generation.

About this book

"I have witnessed first hand the heart and passion that Saulo Santos has for the body of Christ. Especially in seeing people reach their full potential and fulfilling their purpose in God's Kingdom. This book is like the scalpel of a surgeon. Every page will shape your heart to pursue God's plan for your life, especially when you encounter difficulties on your journey. Get Out of Your Hiding Place is a book that will challenge you to get up, get out and move forward in your destiny. This is a must read for those looking to be inspired and uplifted to live and walk by faith, even in the face of life's trials and tribulations."

Robbie Howells
Founder & Senior Pastor of The Warehouse Church, UK.

"The book 'Get out of your hiding place' is challenging. It was written for everyone hungry and thirsty for justice, for all those who don't conform to the sameness in Christian life and want to reach out for more in God.

It is written in clear and simple language, aiming to reach every type of person, from simple to erudite, without tiring the reader.

I recommend it as essential reading."

Tirso de Mello Santos
Agape Church, Ponta Grossa, Brazil

"If you want to read something to take you to God's grand throne room, you have chosen the right book. Here you will find words of peace and joy, messages from the pure heart of a true worshipper.

This is a book written for everyone who wants to come out of formal religion and fly like eagles to reach a deeper intimacy with God."

Vera Lúcia Oliveira Santos
Agape Church, Ponta Grossa, Brazil
Author of the book "Roses in the Wilderness"

"I've had the privilege to know Saulo Oliveira Santos and his family for more than 20 years since he was very young. Even then, we couldn't deny his ministry calling. Even with a very introverted personality, there was a great transformation, noticeable to everyone when he started to worship. The book 'Get out of your hiding place' marks the bloom of a great ministry, which I recognise is very strong in his life and the book describes his experience. It has a very involving narrative and sensibly approaches many moments of his life and ministry. I recommend reading this book because it will certainly build your life and kindle a flame in your spirit, which will ignite your call to ministry. The sensible and challenging narrative will inspire you to get out of 'your' hiding place, whatever it may be. God bless you."

Gabriel Frecceiro
Agape Church, Curitiba, Brazil

"In the pages of this book we can find a living testimony in every written word. The author of this book 'Get out of your hiding place', describes how 'internal and external limitations' can and want to render us unable to do anything for God. Some of these limitations are imposed by our minds, ourselves, the environment we're in, or even by Satan. However, Saulo notes that if we look to the holy scriptures, we may find, like him, characters with which we can identify because they had the same 'limitations and inabilities' that we have. They may even go through seasons of 'failures and trials'. Yet, they were able to fulfil their mission, even going through difficult times and times of learning and transition. They were able to enjoy the blessing from God as a result of a life of perseverance, obedience and experiences with God.

So, I recommend for everyone who loves a good read to dive deep into every word of this book and to be encouraged. Certainly, we all, one way or the other, go through times of 'inferiority complex', or we judge ourselves as 'failures' or 'unable' to do anything for God. In this book, you will find words of motivation to help you make yourself available to be used by God in this season."

Daniel C. Moreira, *Church at Home, London, United Kingdom*

Printed in Great Britain
by Amazon